Studies in Philosophy

Edited by
Robert Nozick
*Pellegrino University Professor
at Harvard University*

Problems of Compositionality

Zoltán Gendler Szabó

Routledge
Taylor & Francis Group

LONDON AND NEW YORK

First Published 2000 by
Garland Publishing Inc.

Published 2013 by Routledge
2 Park Square, Milton Park, Abingdon, Oxfordshire OX14 4RN
711 Third Avenue, New York, NY 10017

First issued in paperback 2014

Routledge is an imprint of the Taylor & Francis Group, an informa business

Copyright © 2000 by Zoltán Gendler Szabó.

All rights reserved. No part of this book may be reprinted or reproduced or utilized in any form or by any electronic, mechanical, or other means, now known or hereafter invented, including photocopying and recording, or in any information storage or retrieval system, without permission in writing from the publishers.

Library of Congress Cataloging-in-Publication Data
Szabó, Zoltán Gendler.
 Problems of compositionality / Zoltán Gendler Szabó.
  pm. — (Studies in philosophy)
 Slightly rev. version of the author's thesis (Massachusetts Institute of Technology—1995).
 Includes bibliographical references and index.
 ISBN 0-8153-3790-6 (alk. paper)
 1. Semantics. 2. Compositionality (Linguistics) I. Title. II. Studies in philosophy (New York, N.Y.)
P325.5.C626 S97 2000
401'.41—dc21   99-054662

ISBN 13: 978-1-138-86839-7 (pbk)
ISBN 13: 978-0-8153-3790-4 (hbk)

Contents

Preface   vii

1. The Principle   3
    1.1 Statement of the Principle   3
    1.2 Alternative Formulations   6
    1.3 Parallelism   9
    1.4 Substitutivity   14
    1.5 Functionality   19
    1.6 Summary   26

2. Linguistic Semantics   27
    2.1 Is Semantics Empirical?   27
    2.2 The First Dogma   32
    2.3 The Second Dogma   39
    2.4 Semantics without Epistemology   46
    2.5 Semantics without Ontology   49
    2.6 The Third Dogma   52
    2.7 Summary   56

3. The Argument   59
    3.1 The Argument from Understanding   59
    3.2 Meaning and Understanding   64
    3.3 The Strong Principle of Understanding   67
    3.4 The Modest Principle of Understanding   73
    3.5 Understanding and the Missing Shade of Blue   81
    3.6 Summary   85

v

4.	Adjectives in Context	87
	4.1 The Context Thesis	87
	4.2 The Color of a Painted Leaf	92
	4.3 Problems with 'Good'	95
	4.4 Ways of Being Good	102
	4.5 Varieties of Incompleteness	105
	4.6 Ways of Being Green?	111
	4.7 Summary	113
5.	Descriptions in Context	115
	5.1 A Parallel	115
	5.2 Referring and Quantifying Phrases	117
	5.3 Two Objections to the Quantificational View	122
	5.4 Replies to Donnellan's Objection	128
	5.5 Replies to Heim's Objection	130
	5.6 Methodological Considerations	134
	5.7 Coreferring Phrases and File-Cards	140
	5.8 Summary	146
6.	In Place of a Conclusion	149
Bibliography		151
Index		161

Preface

A sentence, a clause, or a phrase is a complex entity: it is built up from smaller parts—morphemes and words—in accordance with the rules of grammar. A sentence, clause, or phrase is also a sign: it has some meaning, a role it plays in language and in human interactions. How are complexity and meaning related? The classic answer to this question is that the meaning of a complex expression is *determined by* the meanings of its constituents and its structure: once you fix what the parts mean and how they are put together, you have fixed the meaning of the whole. This is the principle of compositionality, a cornerstone of semantic theorizing perhaps since the Greek grammarian Priscian, but at the very least since the German logician Frege.

Defenders of the principle of compositionality generally appeal to our ability to understand a potentially infinite array of new sentences we have never heard before. There seems to be only one way to account for this curious ability: we must understand these sentences by understanding their parts and their structure. But if this is how we do it, then the meanings of the parts and the structure must jointly determine the meaning of the whole, and hence, the principle of compositionality holds. Opponents of the principle point to the ubiquity of context-sensitivity in human languages: it seems that the very same sentence can mean one thing in one context of use and quite another thing in another. The context-dependence of a sentence is incompatible with compositionality, unless it can be ultimately traced to context-sensitivity of some lexical constituent of the sentence. Many think that the project of locating the source of all context-dependence in the lexicon is hopeless.

viii   *Preface*

The main aim of this dissertation is to undercut both of these arguments. I argue that the principle of compositionality is a substantive empirical hypothesis which cannot be demonstrated or refuted on the basis of quick *quasi-apriori* considerations.

The dissertation has five real chapters and a brief closing section called (perhaps, somewhat misleadingly) 'Chapter 6'. The main aims of Chapter 1 are to show that some of the seemingly equivalent formulations of the compositionality principle carry different commitments and to choose among the competing versions. The formulation I opt for is the claim that the meaning properties of a complex linguistic expression strongly supervene on its constitution properties. The modal force of supervenience is cashed out in terms of quantification over possible human languages; so the thesis entails that if we have two complex expressions which have different meanings despite the fact that they are built from synonymous constituents via the same syntactic operations, then one of them does not belong to *any* possible human language.

In Chapter 2, I raise a familiar skeptical worry concerning the possibility of an empirical semantic theory based entirely on the linguistic competence of ordinary speakers. I argue that if the principle of compositionality is true (along with two other fundamental theses about meaning) then there is a fairly straightforward way to separate a relatively thin semantic theory closely tied to syntax from the extremely ambitious program of providing an explanatory theory about linguistic meaning in general.

In Chapter 3, I address the most common argument for compositionality: that only compositional theories can explain our ability to understand a vast number of expressions we have never heard before. The purported explanation is based on the idea that we understand a complex expression *by* understanding its constituent parts. This is a thesis about the way we come to know the meanings of certain expressions, a claim that is related, but not identical to the compositionality principle. I formulate a strong, a modest and a weak version of the thesis, and I argue that the first two are probably false, and that although the third is true, it is also compatible with non-compositional theories of meaning.

The topic of Chapters 4 and 5 is the question whether compositionality can be reconciled with the context-dependency of various kinds of expressions. I explore the general thesis that whenever

Preface   ix

the meaning of a complex expression depends on the context, its context-dependency can ultimately be traced to some constituent of it. This thesis is a substantive empirical hypothesis about possible human languages; its truth cannot be established by reflection alone. In Chapters 4 and 5, I argue that adequate semantic and pragmatic theories can be given for context-sensitive adjectives and for context-sensitive descriptions which are in conformity with this thesis.

*   *   *

I wrote this dissertation in 1995 and my views have changed somewhat in the meantime. Although I still believe the main tenets of the dissertation and stand behind most of its arguments, a number of its details now strike me as underdeveloped or otherwise problematic. (Highly revised versions of Chapters 1 and 5 are forthcoming in philosophical journals and an expanded version of Chapter 4 is forthcoming in a volume.[1]) In revising the manuscript, I have employed the following dual strategy. In the main text, I have made almost exclusively stylistic changes; only in a handful of cases did I delete or add sentences, and when I did, I tried not to affect the content substantially. (I have, however, taken the liberty of eliminating three outright errors.) All substantive changes are in new footnotes, which are marked by '*'. (So, if a footnote is unmarked, it or a stylistic variant of it appeared in the original dissertation). Most of the marked footnotes add further support to the view defended in the main text or respond to objections I have heard from friends, colleagues, or referees; the remainder spell out ways in which I changed my view since writing the dissertation. References made within the new footnotes have been added to the bibliography, so a handful of papers and books which appeared after 1995 are listed therein.

There were many who helped with this dissertation. My first debt is to the three members of my committee, (the late) George Boolos, Richard Cartwright, and Robert Stalnaker. Each of them read several drafts of the work as a whole, providing detailed comments and objections throughout. I have sought to express my thanks by

---

[1] 'Compositionality as Supervenience' forthcoming in *Linguistics and Philosophy* ,'Descriptions and Uniqueness' forthcoming in *Philosophical Studies,* and 'Adjectives in Context' forthcoming in R. Harmish and I. Kenesei eds. *Festschrift for Ferenc Kiefer.* Amsterdam: John Benjamins.

x   *Preface*

incorporating their suggestions and responding to their doubts, but let me here express more publicly my gratitude to all three of them.

Two other members of the faculty of the Department of Linguistics and Philosophy at MIT—Judith Jarvis Thomson and Irene Heim—also played a vital role in my work on this dissertation. The central argument of chapter 4 originally appeared in a paper which I wrote for a seminar of Judith Jarvis Thomson's; her work on 'good', and her comments on the previous drafts of this chapter shaped my ideas considerably. The argument of chapter 5 was largely motivated by Irene Heim's writings, and by the conversations we had over my four years at MIT. Her comments have helped me to develop the view I hold and the arguments I present in its favor.

For providing me with a stimulating and supportive environment during my time in graduate school, I am grateful to a number of other professors, classmates, and friends at MIT and at Harvard. Among them, I owe specific debts to Ned Block, Sylvain Bromberger, Alex Byrne, Michael Glanzberg, Steven Gross, James Higginbotham, Jason Stanley, and Daniel Stoljar, each of whom shaped my views through extensive conversations and/or detailed comments on parts of this dissertation.

My initial training in philosophy was at the Eötvös Loránd University in Budapest, and I owe thanks to the entire department for what I learned there, especially to Imre Ruzsa, who was my main mentor during my undergraduate education. Much of what I know about semantics, I learned in the old room 13 of the Research Institute for Linguistics in Budapest, primarily from László Kálmán who worked there and László Pólos who (like myself) was usually supposed to be somewhere else. Finally, István Bodnár, scholar of antiquity and careful reader of practically everything that I have ever written, has been for more than a decade a teacher, a colleague, and a friend.

Audiences at my thesis seminar at MIT, at the Research Institute for Linguistics in Budapest, at the Department of Philosophy of Cornell University, at the University of Rochester, and the Summer 1997 Linguistic Institute at Cornell provided me with the opportunity to present parts of this work, and with helpful suggestions and comments that allowed me to refine it. I should especially like to thank my colleagues at Cornell, most of whom read large parts of this thesis and grilled me extensively about its details during my job candidacy in 1995. Their comments and criticism helped me considerably.

Preface xi

Financial support for my work came from three sources. I am grateful to MIT, to the National Scientific and Research Found (OTKA) of Hungary, and to the Soros Foundation for stipends during my graduate career.

In the years since 1995, I have received a host of helpful comments and criticism from a number of colleagues and students. At the risk of omitting someone important, I want to specifically thank Molly Diesing, Kai van Fintel, Harold Hodes, John Hawthorne, Sally McConnell-Ginet, Tom McKay, Jeff Roland, Gabriel Segal, Jason Stanley (again) and Mandy Simons. Jeff Roland also provided superb research support in preparing the volume's index.

Finally, this work could never have been written without Tamar Szabó Gendler; it is not an exaggeration to say that each page bears the imprint of her philosophical and editorial acuity. I am grateful to her for her encouragement, support, friendship, and love.

Problems of Compositionality

CHAPTER 1

The Principle

1. STATEMENT OF THE PRINCIPLE

The phrase 'principle of compositionality', at least as I am using it, refers to the following thesis:

Principle of Compositionality: The meaning of a complex expression is determined by the meanings of its constituents and by its structure.

The principle is not about complex expressions of some specific language, nor is it about complex expressions of any language whatsoever. Rather, it is a general thesis about human languages, like Afghan, Estonian, or Spanish, but not about artificial sign systems, like the language of set theory, secret codes, or programming languages. Languages that evolved naturally, but are more or less dead tongues by now, like Kamas, Latin or Syriac, are intended to be included, as are languages that will evolve from those languages now spoken. The best way to characterize the scope of the tacit universal quantification over languages in the principle of compositionality is to say that the thesis concerns *all possible human languages*. A possible human language is a language suitable for the expression and communication of thoughts that can be learned by human beings under normal social conditions as a first language.[1] Exactly which languages are possible human languages is, of course, an open question.

---

[1] * The language of pure set theory and the language of traffic signs are not possible human languages because they violate the first condition: they are not suitable for the expression and communication of a wide range of thoughts. A language whose

3

4 *Problems of Compositionality*

The principle of compositionality is widely endorsed by linguists and philosophers. This is a remarkable fact, given the extent of general disagreement concerning the fundamental principles of semantics.[2] Unfortunately, the harmony of opinions does not extend much beyond bare approval. According to some, the principle concerns our cognitive makeup, and consequently it belongs to psychology; others argue that it concerns the relationship between syntax and semantics, and therefore it is in the domain of linguistics. It has been suggested that the principle is a trivial platitude, a significant empirical hypothesis, a methodological assumption, a powerful philosophical thesis in need of a deep argument, and so on. The differences strongly suggest that the agreement about the truth of the principle is chimerical: almost everyone seems to have a different interpretation in mind.

The elusiveness of the principle derives from the three crucial concepts it involves: meaning, structure, and determination. It is impossible to give a detailed characterization of these concepts, but to avoid trivial misunderstandings, it might be useful to say something about them in advance.

The *meaning* of an expression is a feature or property of it in virtue of which it has its role in a language, i.e. in virtue of which it can contribute to the expression and communication of thoughts. Meaningless expressions have no role, and consequently one cannot use them correctly or incorrectly. This is not to say that one cannot do anything with such expressions, only that their use is quite unpredictable. Expressions that have the same meaning in a language play the same role in the language, though not necessarily in the same

---

expressions are at least a hundred phonemes long, or a language with only two phonemes are not possible human languages because they violate the second condition: the expressions of the former language would be too hard to keep in mind, while the expressions of the latter would be too easy to confuse with one another.

[2] * Not that semantic theories are usually compositional; it is often more convenient to present one's findings without worrying much about this principle. What matters is the tacit commitment that in the final analysis the non-compositional wrinkles can be ironed out. A nice example of the way this conviction influences semantics is the fate of Discourse Representation Theory. Kamp (1981) proposed DRT in part as a solution to problems of anaphora; he argued that the full range of data about syntactically unbound pronouns cannot be accommodated within a compositional framework. The response to this claim was overwhelming: in the subsequent years several compositional theories have been proposed which could do as much or more than the original DRT in dealing with syntactically unbound anaphora: cf. among many others, Zeevat (1989), Groenendijk and Stokhoff (1991), Muskens (1994), Dekker (1994), van Eijk and Kamp (1997).

The Principle 5

way. One might understand roles in a language on analogy with roles in a play. A meaningless expression is like an actor who has no role in the performance. He might interfere by jumping onto the stage, and his interference might even be quite significant, but this does not make his actions part of the play. Synonymous expressions are like actors playing the same role, say, on different days. One might do the job better than the other, but only insofar as he performs the same role in a better way.

An expression is complex if it is constructed from simpler ones by application of certain rules of composition. The *structure* of the expression is the way the expression is syntactically combined from simpler expressions, called constituents. The structure of a complex expression might be characterized by a certain sequence of rule-applications which show how the expression is generated from its constituents. Analogously, one could say that the structure of a chemical compound is characterized by a sequence of reactions through which it is generated from its constituents.[3]

The claim that certain properties *determine* certain others has a modal character: it says that two things cannot differ in terms of the latter properties, unless they differ in terms of the former as well. Understood in this way, the principle of compositionality amounts to the thesis that two expressions cannot have different meanings, unless they also differ either in terms of the meanings of their constituents, or

---

[3] * What I said about linguistic meaning and structure puts very weak constraints on these notions. This is as it should be: the principle of compositionality is an extremely general principle which is supposed to be compatible with widely different conceptions of meaning and structure. But we do need to place *some* constraints. Zadrozny (1994) proves that given a set S of strings generated from an arbitrary alphabet via concatenation and a meaning function m which assigns the members of an arbitrary set M to the members of S, we can construct a new meaning function μ such that for all $s, t \in S$ $\mu(st) = \mu(s)(\mu(t))$ and $\mu(s)(s) = m(s)$. (The values of μ are functions whose values are defined using the so-called Solution Lemma, which is provable in the theory of non-wellfounded sets.) Let us accept for a moment that fulfillment of the first of these conditions guarantees compositionality. (I will actually argue against this claim later.) Then the theorem shows that an arbitrary meaning assignment can be imitated compositionally. Of course, if we reject that complex expressions of human languages could have such a primitive syntax and such fanciful meanings, we can deny that μ is a meaning assignment. So, if we accept the minimal constraints I proposed, Zadrozny's result poses no direct threat to the empirical significance of compositionality. For a similar assessment, see Kazmi and Pelletier (1998) and Westerståhl (1998).

6 *Problems of Compositionality*

in their structure.[4] The analogous claim for the valence of chemical compounds is the following plausible claim: two molecules cannot differ in their valences, unless they also differ either in the valences of their constituents, or in their structure.[5]

My aim in the first chapter of the dissertation is to make clear what the principle of compositionality is. To achieve this, I will say something about what it is not: I will look at some other principles, which are often—but if I am correct mistakenly—taken to be equivalent formulations. [6]

2. ALTERNATIVE FORMULATIONS

It is often suggested that the principle of compositionality has several alternative formulations. The following examples come from a recent book on logic and language:[7]

(1) The principle of compositionality [...] requires that the meaning (and thus the truth value) of a composite sentence depends only on the meanings (truth values) of the sentences of which it is composed.[8]

---

[4] * This formulation leaves the nature of the modality quite open. I will return to this issue in section 5.

[5] The analogy is from Field (1972), pp. 362 - 3. The use of chemistry as an analogy in talking about compositionality goes back to Frege. Cf. Frege (1891), pp. 135 - 6, Frege (1892), p. 182, Frege (1906a), p. 302, and Frege (1914), pp. 208 - 9.

[6] * The prevailing attitude towards these alternatives seems to be *laissez fair*: anyone is entitled to his or her compositionality and the question which of these is supposed to be the correct reading of the principle is postponed until we know more about semantics. This strategy has its merits; science often proceeds by bracketing foundational questions. Still, a bit more clarity would be useful here. My methodology will be the *reverse* of the usual one. Instead of formulating a more precise version of the principle of compositionality outright and judging the compositionality of various languages using the stipulated clarification, I will assume that, at least in simple cases, we have intuitions about whether a particular language is compositional and then I exploit these intuitions in understanding what the principle says. Semanticists are used to rely on intuitions when arguing about the meaning of various sentences; I suggest that they do the same in trying to find out how best to interpret the principle of compositionality. The reading I will propose differs from the standard interpretations. My claim is not that the principle *must* be understood in the way I will suggest; it is simply that my reading fits better than others with our – not entirely pretheoretical, but still, reasonably innocent – intuitions about what it is for a language to be compositional.

[7] Gamut (1991). The book was written by a team of Dutch logicians, linguists, and philosophers from *G*roeningen, *Am*sterdam, and *U*trecht. Hence the acronym.

[8] Gamut (1991), Vol. 1, p. 28.

The Principle 7

(2) [...] the meaning of a composite expression must be built up from the meanings of its composite parts. This principle, which is generally attributed to Frege, is known as *the principle of the compositionality of meaning*.[9]

(3) [Sentences] can get a semantic interpretation simply by interpreting the basic sentences and then giving a semantic parallel to the syntactic construction steps. [...] This insight of Frege is now called *the principle of compositionality of meaning*, or *Frege's principle*.[10]

(4) If two expressions have the same reference, then substitution of one for the other in a third expression does not change its reference.
If two expressions have the same sense, then substitution of one for the other in a third expression does not change its sense.
[...] The two principles are also known as *principles of compositionality*, of reference and sense, respectively.[11]

(5) [...] the interpretation of a complex expression is a *function* of the interpretations of its parts. This is the principle of compositionality of meaning, also referred to as 'Frege's principle.'[12]

I think none of these principles is equivalent to the principle of compositionality as stated in the previous section. Some of the differences are trivial, others are rather instructive. I will run through the trivial ones first, modify the principles accordingly, and then turn to the more substantive issues.

The first thing to notice is that (1) and (3) are about sentences, so they can only be regarded as restricted versions of the principle of compositionality. They concern only complex sentences in so far as they have simpler sentences as constituents. (2) is about all composite expressions, but in stating it the authors had presumably only sentences in mind: this is why it speaks only about composite parts. If we replace 'sentence' by 'expression' in (1) and (3), and 'composite parts' with

---

[9] Gamut (1991), Vol. 1, pp. 5 - 6.
[10] Gamut (1991), Vol. 1, p. 15.
[11] Gamut (1991), Vol. 2, pp. 11 - 2.
[12] Gamut (1991), Vol. 2, p. 140.

8   *Problems of Compositionality*

'constituents' in (2), we get principles of full generality. (For the sake of uniformity, we can also replace 'composite expression' by 'complex' in (1) and (2), and 'parts' by 'constituents' in (5).)

(4) mentions two principles, the first of which is not about meaning. The parenthetical remarks in (1) can also be regarded as announcements of a different, but related principle, which the authors call 'compositionality of reference'. We can disregard that thesis here.

The second principle in (4) talks about 'sense'. Although 'sense' might mean something that is either more or less comprehensive than 'meaning'. For the purposes of this discussion, 'sense' in (4) will be replaced by 'meaning'.[13] The term 'interpretation', which occurs in (3) and (5), can be understood as referring to the process of interpreting an expression, or as referring to what gets assigned to the expression as a result of this process. In (3) 'semantic interpretation' will be understood as the process of meaning assignment, whereas in (5) it will be read as 'meaning'.[14]

Finally, (1) and (5) obviously cannot be true as stated. The meaning of a composite expression cannot depend only on (or be a function of) the meanings of the expressions of which it is composed. Presumably 'John is taller than Bill' and 'Bill is taller than John' have

---

[13] Frege, who introduced the term 'Sinn' which gets translated as 'sense', did not identify senses with conventional linguistic meanings. On the one hand, different expressions with the same sense might bring different associations, and hence, they might have quite different stylistic value. Consequently, a lexical entry might distinguish expressions that have the same sense. On the other hand, conventional linguistic meanings are usually vague, but senses are not. So, expressions may have the same foggy conventional linguistic meaning, and still differ in their senses. Cf. Burge (1990), esp. pp. 40 - 1. Fregean senses are essentially different from meanings, if the latter are construed according to the model of intuitively acceptable *explications* of the role an expression plays in a language. However, whether such a notion of conventional linguistic meaning is really what semantics is after seems to me to be quite dubious. Many linguists and philosophers have suggested that the meanings studied in semantics are more like Frege's senses than like dictionary entries. This is certainly the view of the Gamut authors. I will return to the question concerning the relation between the Fregean sense and the conception of meaning relevant in linguistics in Section 3 of Chapter 2, and in Section 3 of Chapter 3.

[14] 'Interpretation' can be taken as a general term for anything that the semantics assigns to an expression. If read in this broad manner, (5) may comprise also the principle that is called in (4) 'principle of compositionality of reference'. In their discussion of propositional logic the Gamut authors occasionally use the term 'meaning' in a similarly broad sense; this explains the parenthetical remarks in (1).

The Principle 9

the same constituents, but they are clearly not synonyms.[15] Besides the meanings of the constituents, their meaning depends on the structure of the expression as well.

Making all the trivial changes in the quotes we get the following principles:

(1′) The meaning of a complex expression depends only on the meanings of the expressions of which it is composed and on its structure.

(2′) The meaning of a complex expression must be built up from the meanings of its constituents.

(3′) Expressions can be assigned meanings simply by assigning meaning to the basic expressions and then giving a semantic parallel to the syntactic construction steps.

(4′) If two expressions have the same meaning, then substitution of one for the other in a third expression does not change its meaning.

(5′) The meaning of a complex expression is a function of the meanings of its constituents and of its structure.

I think (1') is a stylistic variant of the principle of compositionality as stated in the previous section. All the others, however, say something quite different. I will try to show this in the following three sections.

3. PARALLELISM

In an unpublished note to Ludwig Darmstaedter, Frege gave expression to an important principle concerning the relationship between thoughts and sentences. He wrote that "corresponding to the whole-part relation of a thought and its parts we have, by and large, the same relation for the sentence and its parts."[16] Thoughts, which are the senses of certain sentences, have a structure similar to the sentences themselves: as a

---

[15] I use the term 'synonym' in a slightly broader sense than the usual. Normally we only speak about words as being synonymous to one another. I mean by 'synonymy' the relation of meaning identity between expressions: words, phrases, sentences, sequences of sentences, etc.

[16] Frege (1919), p. 255. Cf. also Frege (1906b), p. 192 and Frege (1892), p. 193.

10   *Problems of Compositionality*

sentence is built up from its basic constituents, the sense of the sentence is constructed from the senses of the constituents.

Russellian propositions are in one respect similar to Fregean thoughts: they are complex entities whose structure corresponds more or less to the structure of sentences that express them. The crucial difference is that the Russellian proposition expressed by a sentence is built from the referents of the words occurring in the sentence, while the Fregean thought expressed by the a sentence is built from the senses of the words. The Russellian proposition expressed by the sentence 'Mont Blanc is more than 4000 meters high' contains Mont Blanc with "all its snowfields" as a constituent.[17]

Some philosophers hold Fregean or Russellian views about the nature of meanings of complex expressions and endorse (2′).[18] This is a thesis that implies compositionality: if the meaning of a complex expression is built up from the meanings of its constituents, then surely what the meanings of constituents are and how they are put together determines what the meaning of the complex is. However, (2′) requires something beyond compositionality. (2′) says that the meaning of complex expressions must itself be complex. According to (2′) nothing could count as meaning for a complex expression, unless it has other meanings as parts. I will call (2') the *strong principle of parallelism*.[19]

As far as compositionality goes, the meaning of a complex expression could easily be something unstructured. Take for example a simple and naive intensional semantics, where the meaning of 'Peter' is

---

[17] Russell (1904), p. 169.

[18] For example Cresswell (1985), p. 25 - 31 and Jackendoff (1983), p. 76. The situation is often more complicated. For example, Kaplan (1977) distinguishes between two notions of meaning: the content and the character. The content of a sentence is a complex built from the referents of the constituent expressions, while the character is a function that assigns to each context of utterance the content of the sentence uttered in that context. The principle of parallelism holds for the first of these notions, but not for the second.

[19] * When I interpret (2′) in this manner, I take the building metaphor very seriously. It is quite clear that many authors who have formulated the principle of compositionality as (2′) do not do so. Perhaps all they intend to express by (2′) is the claim that there is a function from the meanings of parts to the meanings of wholes. It is sometimes suggested (e.g. Salmon (1989), p. 438) that Frege himself intended only this much. In 'Compound Thoughts' Frege acknowledges that "we really talk figuratively when we transfer the relation of whole and part to thoughts; yet the analogy is so ready to hand and so generally appropriate that we are hardly even bothered by the hitches which occur from time to time." Frege (1923), p. 390. It is, however, quite clear that Frege rejects only the spatial connotations of the part/whole idiom. The idea that thoughts are structured is not a mere metaphor for him.

The Principle 11

a function which assigns Peter to each possible world where he exists, the meaning of 'is asleep' is another function which assigns to each possible world the set of things that are asleep there, and the meaning of 'Peter is asleep' is the set of possible worlds where this sentence is true. The structure of the sentence is subject-predicate, which corresponds in the semantics to the relation R, defined as follows: fRg is true in w if and only if $f(w) \in g(w)$. Then the meanings of 'Peter' and 'is asleep' together with the structure of the sentence determine the meaning of 'Peter is asleep'. However, there is nothing in the set of possible worlds where Peter is asleep that could directly correspond to the meanings of the constituents of the sentence. This semantics is compositional, but it clearly violates the strong principle of parallelism.[20]

The chemical analogy mentioned in the first section is useful here. The valence of a molecule is determined by the valences of its constituent atoms and by the structure of the molecule, but it is certainly false that the valence of a molecule is built up from the valences of its constituents.[21]

So, it is certainly not true that the strong principle of parallelism is equivalent to the principle of compositionality. I suspect that the misunderstanding originates from a certain formulation of the compositionality principle. One could say that the meaning of a complex expression is determined by the meanings of its constituents and the way *they* are combined. The question is what the antecedent of the pronoun 'they' is supposed to be. If 'they' corefers with 'its constituents', this formulation is equivalent to the principle of compositionality. If 'they' corefers with 'the meanings of its constituents', the formulation says the same as the strong principle of parallelism.

(3′) is a formulation that does not speak of meanings as being built up of other meanings, but it still captures some of the intuition behind

---

[20] The same holds for the intensions of Carnap and Montague. They are unstructured entities and hence they cannot be regarded as fully adequate theoretical reconstructions for Fregean senses.

[21] * This means that if we think of meanings as properties of expressions, rather than as complex objects associated with the expressions, then (2′) loses much of its intuitive appeal. And it is easy to think of meanings in this way; all we have to do is transform claims of the form 'expression e is associated with its meaning m' into 'expression e has the property of having m as its meaning'.

12   *Problems of Compositionality*

(2′). It requires that the assignment of meaning to any complex expression should mirror the way the expression itself is built up from its simpler constituents. I will call (3′) the *weak principle of parallelism*. To illustrate what is meant by the weak principle of parallelism, here is another quote:

> One important characteristic of the semantic interpretation process [...] is that strict parallelism is maintained between the syntactic constructions and the semantic interpretations. [...] There is a methodological consideration underlying this practice, one which can be traced back to Frege. This German logician and mathematician gave the first satisfactory analysis of sentences with relational predicates and multiple quantification in 1879, in his *Begriffschrift*. Now the fundamental insight behind his solution to these age-old problems is that every sentence, no matter how complex, is the result of a systematic construction process which builds it up step by step, and in which every step can receive a semantic interpretation. This is the well-known *principle of semantic compositionality*.[22]

This is a requirement that is respected by the simple possible worlds semantics mentioned above, or by almost any formal semantic framework.[23] Weak parallelism entails compositionality: if one can assign the meaning to a complex expression by starting from the meanings of its constituents and then applying the semantic rules at each step parallel to the syntactic composition of the expression, then the meaning of the complex expression is obviously determined by the meanings of the constituents and the structure of the expression.[24] But the principle of weak parallelism says more than the principle of compositionality.

The principle of compositionality could hold for a language that does not have a meaning assignment that is strictly parallel to its syntax. Consider, for example, the possibility that in the construction of some complex expressions, certain intermediary steps yield

---

[22] Gamut (1991), Vol. 2, pp. 4 - 5.

[23] A notable exception is Hintikka's game theoretic semantics. For Hintikka's arguments against parallelism see Hintikka (1981).

[24] * This is not obvious. Given the notion of determination I defend in Section 5 of this chapter, weak parallelism does not curtail compositionality. Assuming a weaker notion it does.

The Principle
13

representations that have *no meaning* whatsoever. What if the correct syntax of English is such that in generating the sentence 'Peter is asleep' the last step is joining 'Peter is' with 'asleep'? 'Peter is' is not an expression of English, so it makes little sense to assign meaning to it. Still, it is perfectly possible that even in this language the meanings of constituent expressions ('Peter', 'is', 'asleep', but not 'Peter is') and the way they are combined by the syntax determine the meaning of 'Peter is asleep'.[25] The analogy with valence is again useful. Imagine that some molecules are generated from their primitive constituents in such a way that there are certain intermediary entities for which the chemical property of valence is not even defined. Then we could not have a valence assignment to molecules and atoms which would parallel the generation of some molecules. Still, it would be true that the valence of any molecule is determined by the valences of its constituents and by its structure.

What is at issue with regard to parallelism is the thesis called *autonomy of syntax*. Some semanticists deny that there is such a thing as the correct syntax of a natural language independent of semantic considerations. They claim that it is always possible to give a rule-to-rule semantics, since one can choose the syntax freely. One should make the choice then in such a way that makes a parallel semantics possible.

I do not know whether this view is correct. The important point is that even if syntax is completely autonomous, and even if there is no guarantee that there can be strict parallelism between syntax and semantics, the principle of compositionality can still be true. Construing the question of compositionality as being about the autonomy of syntax is misleading.

The conclusion of this section is that both the strong and the weak principles of parallelism are stronger theses than the principle of compositionality. The meanings of a complex expression might be

---

[25] * It is important to mention that this argument relies on a weak reading of the compositionality principle. According to the *strong reading* of the principle, the meaning of a complex expression is determined by the meanings of its *immediate* constituents and the way those are combined; according to the *weak reading*, the meaning of a complex expression is determined by the meanings of its *ultimate* constituents and the way those are combined. The weak reading allows for the possibility that some of the constituents of a complex expression are meaningless, as long as the meaningless constituents are themselves complex and their ultimate constituents have meaning. (2′) is *not* stronger than the strong reading of the principle of compositionality.

14   *Problems of Compositionality*

determined by the meanings of its constituents and its structure, even if the interpretation does not follow the way the compound expression is built from its simple parts.

4. SUBSTITUTIVITY

Let me restate (4′) from section 2 here as the *principle of substitutivity*:[26]

Principle of Substitutivity: If two expressions have the same meaning, then substitution of one for the other in a third expression does not change the meaning of the third expression.

This is a crucial thesis, often used in arguing *against* various conceptions of meaning. Take for example the idea that the role a proper name can play in language (and hence its meaning) is completely exhausted by its having a certain referent. This implies (together with the *prima facie* innocent assumption that 'Mark Twain' and 'Samuel Clemens' are proper names referring to the same individual) that 'John believes that Mark Twain was American' and 'John believes that Samuel Clemens was American' are synonymous, which seems clearly false. Or consider the idea that the meaning of a predicate expression is its intension: a function from possible worlds to its extension at those worlds. This implies (together with the compelling assumption that 'is the sum of the first 100 natural numbers' and 'is the sum of 5000 and 50' are predicate expressions having the same intension) that 'John believes that 5050 is the sum of the first 100 natural numbers' and 'John believes that 5050 is the sum of 5000 and 50' are synonymous, which sounds absurd. The arguments obviously use the principle of substitutivity as a tacit premise.

Such arguments may seem simple and persuasive,[27] but the appeal to substitutivity in them cannot be replaced—as it is frequently

---

[26] * In the philosophical literature the name 'principle of substitutivity' is usually reserved for the thesis that if two singular terms are coreferential then substitution of one for the other in a sentence is truth-preserving.

[27] * It is far from obvious whether such arguments can *prove* that co-referring proper names or coextensional predicates cannot be substituted for one another in belief contexts *salva veritate*. As the puzzle of Pierre shows, analogous difficulties can be stated without appeal to substitutivity. Cf. Kripke (1979). This may encourage some to bite the bullet

The Principle 15

assumed—by an appeal to compositionality. As I will argue, the two principles are independent.

It is quite trivial that one cannot get compositionality from substitutivity. Any language that contains *no synonyms* trivially conforms to the principle of substitutivity, but some of these languages are obviously non-compositional. This observation brings us quite far, since it reveals how easy it is to construct examples of non-compositional languages that conform to substitutivity. Suppose L_1 is a language where any substitution of synonyms within a third expression leaves the meaning of the third expression unchanged. Let L_1^+ be an extension of L_1 with some complex expression c and its constituents e_1, ... , e_n. Let us suppose that c is constructed from e_1, ... , e_n using the syntactic rules of L_1, and that the meaning of c in L_1^+ is *not* determined by the meanings of e_1, ... , e_n in L_1^+. This means that L_1^+ violates the principle of compositionality. But if we also assume that the expressions e_1, ... , e_n have no synonyms in L_1 or among each other, L_1^+ conforms to the principle of substitutivity. [28]

Even assuming that *all* expressions have synonyms, substitutivity does not yield compositionality. Imagine a language L_2 where each expression has many synonyms, and which conforms to the principle of substitutivity. Let L_2' be a language obtained from L_2 through a slight modification: the meanings of subsentential expressions and the syntactic rules remain the same, but the meanings of sentences in L_2' depend on their first letter. [29] If it is 'A', the meaning of the sentence in

---

and insist that, despite appearances, the substitution pairs in the above paragraph have the same truth-value.

[28] * The claim that L_1^+ violates the principle of compositionality heavily relies on the ordinary meaning of 'determine'. I think in the present context, when our aim is to understand what the principle of compositionality says, such a reliance is legitimate. Let me use an example to illustrate my point. Suppose we have a population where everybody has different genes. I take it that it would not be trivial whether in this population genes determine eye-color. And I take it that it is not incoherent to suggest that we might refute the hypothesis that eye color is thus determined by finding an individual whose eye-color depends partly on non-genetic factors. Somebody who would object to this by saying "Look, all I meant by the claim that genes determine eye-color was that there are no two people with the same genes and different eye-colors" could be legitimately rebuffed by saying that he does not use the word 'determine' in its normal sense. Similarly, those who argue that the meaning of c is determined compositionally (because in L^+ no other expression has the same structure and constituents with the same meaning) must have a rather unusual sense of 'determine' in mind.

[29] Here, and throughout the dissertation I will say that if language L and language L' have the same expressions interpreted differently, they are different languages. In this, I follow

L_2' is the meaning of the negation of the sentence in L_2; if it is any other letter, then the meaning of the sentence is the same in L_2' as in L_2. (For example, if L_2 were English, the meaning of 'An elephant is walking in the park' in L_2' would be that no elephant is walking in the park, and the meaning of 'Every elephant is walking in the park' would be that every elephant is walking in the park.) Assume that L_2 does contain sentences that start with the letter 'A', i.e. that L_2' and L_2 are indeed different. Then L_2' violates the principle of compositionality: the meanings of sentences whose first letter is 'A' are not determined by the meanings of the constituents and their way of composition. At the same time L_2' can easily conform to the principle of substitutivity: all we need is a contingent fact about L_2, namely, that the set of expressions whose first letter is 'A' be closed under synonymy. So, for example, if L_2 contains the word 'apple' all the synonyms of 'apple' also have 'a' as their first letter, if L_2 contains the sentence 'Aristotle was bald' all the sentences that mean the same as 'Aristotle was bald' start with the letter 'A', etc. Then it remains true in L_2' that no substitution of synonyms can change the meaning of the expression in which the substitution took place.[30]

The mistaken belief that substitutivity entails compositionality is based on an illusion: that if in a language substitution of synonyms within a complex expression preserves the meaning of the complex expressions, the only conceivable reason for this would be that the language is compositional. The examples of L_1^+ and L_2' show that the reason might be something much more complicated. If the principle of substitutivity holds for some language, this may *suggest* that the language is compositional, but such a consequence cannot be drawn on logical grounds.

The situation is not better with regard to the other direction of the alleged equivalence. Compositionality does not entail substitutivity. Suppose someone suggests that (6) and (7) have the same meaning in English:[31]

David Lewis: "What is a language? Something which assigns meanings to certain strings of sounds or of marks. It could therefore be a function, a set of ordered pairs of strings and meanings." Lewis (1975b), p. 163.

[30] * As the previous argument, this one also depends on construing 'determine' in the principle of compositionality in a way that is compatible with its ordinary meaning.

[31] The example is due to Peter Geach. Cf. Geach (1965), p. 110.

The Principle 17

(6) Plato was bald.

(7) Baldness was an attribute of Plato.

There are a number of reasonable ways to argue against this position. One can, for example, point out that there are many who would understand (6), but not knowing what attributes are, would be unable to interpret (7). One can point out that (6) is primarily a claim about Plato, whereas (7) seems to be primarily about baldness. Whether these are good arguments is beside the point. The following, however, is certainly a *bad* argument. Assume compositionality, and consider (8). Substituting (7) for (6) in (8) yields (9), which certainly does not mean the same as (8):

(8) The philosopher whose most eminent pupil was Plato was bald.

(9) The philosopher whose most eminent pupil was baldness was an attribute of Plato.

The problem with this argument is, of course, that (6) is not a constituent expression of (8). Compositionality does not guarantee that substituting any *e* by a synonymous *e′* within *c* preserves the meaning of *c*: *e* must at least be a constituent of *c*.

So, perhaps the principle of substitutivity has to be modified in such a way that it requires the expression for which a synonymous expression is substituted in a third expression to be a constituent expression.[32] Unfortunately, such trivial amendment does not help: this improved version still does not follow from the principle of compositionality.

Suppose someone suggested that the expressions 'is not related' and 'is unrelated' are synonymous. Her opponent might point to the fact that the sentences (10) and (11) definitely do not mean the same thing, despite the fact that 'is not related' and 'is unrelated' seem to be constituents in (10) and (11), respectively.

(10) John is not related to everybody.

---

[32] One could modify the terminology, instead of the principle: *replacement* of an expression with another one within a third counts as *substitution* only if the first expression is a constituent of the third. If one understands substitutivity in this way, the objection does not apply.

18   *Problems of Compositionality*

(11) John is unrelated to everybody.

But such an argument would not be convincing. Intuitively, the difference between the two sentences is a structural one, and it should not be attributed to differences in meaning between 'is not related' and 'is unrelated'. Using some formalism, the first sentence can be understood as (10'), while the second can be understood as (11'):

(10') $\forall x(person(x) \rightarrow \neg John\ is\ related\ to(x))$

(11') $\neg\forall x(person(x) \rightarrow John\ is\ related\ to(x))$

The problem is that we have no guarantee that the substitution of a constituent in a complex expression will preserve its structure. If it is possible that the substitution of 'is unrelated to' for 'is not related to' affects the way the constituents of the sentence are put together, the difference in meaning between (10) and (11) does not show that the crucial constituents are not synonymous.[33]

The mistaken belief that compositionality entails substitutivity rests on the idea that all languages resemble simple formal languages. In simple formal languages, the syntax is given by a recursive set of rules, and the interpretation follows the syntactic construction of complex expressions step by step. Under this conception, the question of how a complex expression is built up is completely independent of which words occur in it. So, if a substitution is legitimate, it cannot change the structure of the expression.[34] Now, it might be that natural languages resemble formal languages in this regard. However, it has to be kept in mind that such a resemblance is non-trivial, and moreover, not fully supported by pretheoretical observations.

---

[33] * Another nice example in the same vein is the following fallacy: Since 'Eve is the mother of Cain' is true and 'Eve's elder son was Cain' is true, therefore 'The mother of Cain's elder son was Cain.' The problem here is that in parsing the expression 'the mother of Cain's elder son', the bracketing [the mother of Cain's][elder son] is syntactically forbidden. This example is from Fine (1989), p. 221.

[34] * One might react to these difficulties by *defining* substitution in such a way that a non structure-preserving replacement of one expression by another within a third would not count as substitution. This would have the unfortunate consequence that the innocent notion of substitution would become theoretically loaded: we no longer have a test to decide whether a particular sentence is the result of a substitution within another one. But if we are willing to accept the price, we get a version of the principle of substitutivity which *does* follow from the principle of compositionality.

The Principle

The conclusion of this section is that the principle of substitutivity and the principle of compositionality are independent theses.

5. FUNCTIONALITY

(5') is used by most philosophers and linguists as an equivalent formulation of the principle of compositionality. I will call (5') the *principle of functionality.*

Principle of Functionality: The meaning of a complex expression is a function of the meanings of its constituents and the way these are combined.

The claim that the As are a function of the Bs means that there is a one-many relation f between the As and the Bs, i.e. that there are no Bs that are f-related to more than one A.[35] So, one can rephrase the principle of functionality by saying that expressions combined in the same way from synonymous expressions are themselves synonymous.

It is obvious that the principle of functionality is a consequence of the principle of compositionality. If all meanings are determined by lexical and structural properties, then there cannot be cases when lexically and structurally unambiguous expressions have more than one meaning. What I will argue is that the converse fails to hold.

The failure is surprisingly trivial. Let L be a rich compositional fragment of English which contains the sentences 'Elephants are gray', and 'Julius Caesar was murdered on the ides of March'. Let the function that assigns meanings to expressions of L be g. L' is a language with the same expressions as L, but a different interpretation. The meanings of the expressions in L' can be obtained from the corresponding meanings in L via some permutation p. p leaves every meaning as it is in English, except that it exchanges the meanings of sentences synonymous with 'Elephants are gray' and the meanings of sentences synonymous with 'Julius Caesar was murdered on the ides of March'. L' is interpreted in accordance with the principle of functionality: there is a function g' which assigns meanings to the

---

[35] * Of course, one can interpret the expression 'function of' in the principle of functionality differently. Throughout the following discussion, I will assume this strict mathematical understanding of the claim that something is a function of something else.

20 *Problems of Compositionality*

expressions of L'. For any expression e of L', $g'(e) = p(g(e))$. On the other hand, *if* the sentence 'Elephants are gray' is a genuine complex expression in L', L' violates the principle of compositionality. The assumption that L' is compositional implies that the meanings of 'elephant' and 'gray' plus pluralization and predication determine the meaning of 'Julius Caesar was murdered on the ides of March' in L, and hence *in English* as well, which is absurd.[36]

But can we not simply say that 'Elephants are gray' is *not* a genuine complex expression, but rather an *idiom* of L'?[37] If it were an idiom, it would be a simple expression whose syntactic complexity is semantically irrelevant. But this is not the case. The meanings of the constituent expressions *do* play a role in determining the meaning of the sentence, although they are not *sufficient*. We start from the meanings of 'elephant' and 'gray' in L'. First we apply the inverse of p to these, and we obtain the meanings of 'elephant' and 'gray' in L. Then we apply the syntactic rules, which together with these meanings determine the meaning of the sentence 'Elephants are gray' in L. Finally, we apply p to this meaning, and this gives us the meaning of 'Elephants are gray' in L', i.e. that Julius Caesar was murdered on the ides of March. We can interpret L' via L using p and its inverse as

---

[36] * One might object that this argument is question-begging. All I have shown is that the meaning of certain sentences are determined through *different* functions in L and L'. How would that entail a violation of the principle of compositionality? What I wanted to prove was that functionality does not entail compositionality, but here I seem to rely on the assumption that compositionality demands something beyond there being *some* function in L' which assigns meanings to complex expressions in terms of the meanings of their constituents and their structure. But I don't think that the argument is circular. What I rely on is not the conclusion, it is the ordinary meaning of the word 'determine'. Consider the following example. I take it that if we found two people with the same genes and different eye colors, that would amount to a refutation of the thesis that genes determine eye color. Now, someone might respond to the counterexample thus: "Look, all I mean by genes determining eye color is that for each individual, there is *some* function from her genes to her eye color, so your example does not refute my thesis." The proper answer would be this: "Well, if *that* is what you mean by 'determine', I agree. Unfortunately, that is not what 'determine' means in English. What the counterexample refutes is the claim that genes determine eye color, as determination is ordinarily understood." My answer is exactly analogous.

[37] * Thanks to Bob Stalnaker for the objection. One occasionally encounters the claim that the presence of idioms in a natural language shows that the language is not compositional. That is not necessarily the case. As long as it is theoretically acceptable to treat idioms as simple expressions with semantically spurious syntactic complexity, idioms pose no danger to compositionality. For a detailed discussion of how to accommodate idioms within a compositional theory see Nunberg, Sag and Wasow (1994).

The Principle 21

translation functions. Given the way the example is set up, it is hard to reject the claim that 'Elephants are gray' is a complex expression in L' and that its meaning is not determined merely by the meanings of its constituents and the way they are combined.[38]

Reflection on this example can help explain why the principle of functionality is weaker than the principle of compositionality. If we do not know about L and its relation to L' the fact that the interpretation of L' conforms to the principle of functionality seems to be a curious accident. The claim that the meaning of a whole is determined by the meanings of its parts plus their way of combining says that the meaning of a whole is a function of the meanings of its parts and their way of combining, and that this *must* be so.

Let me elaborate on the modality involved here. The principle of functionality can be regarded as a claim that establishes some connection between two families of properties. The properties belonging to the first family are properties of *having such-and-such meaning*; I call these meaning-properties. The second family contains properties of *having constituents with such-and-such meanings combined in such-and-such way*; I call these constitution-properties. Two expressions are indistinguishable in terms of their meaning properties iff they are synonymous; they are indistinguishable in terms

---

[38] * One might object that my characterization of idioms is unfair: it is not a necessary feature of idioms that their constituents play absolutely no role in determining their meaning. But even if this is granted, understanding an idiom requires *specific* knowledge about the expression beyond its structure and the meaning of its constituents. This explains why we have to learn idioms one by one, which in turn explains why there are relatively few idioms in languages we can learn. However, one could define another language, L^∞ using a permutation function p^∞ which changes the meanings of infinitely many English sentences. Let us say, for example, that the permutation function p^∞ leaves the meaning of every expression unaltered, except that it switches the meaning of sentences synonymous with 'There are two times N apples on the table' with the meaning of sentences synonymous with 'There are two times N plus one apples on the table', where N is a schematic letter for the numeral whose denotation is the natural number n. Speakers of English can easily understand L^∞. (In fact, you have already mastered it by the time you are reading this sentence.) Since we do not think that one can pick up (and so quickly!) a language with infinitely many idioms, we are forced to reject the idea that all sentences whose meanings are not mapped to themselves by p^∞ are idioms of L^∞. By parity of reasoning, we should reject the suggestion that 'Elephants are gray' is an idiom of L': if such a suggestion does not work in general against the type of argument I made, why try it in the specific case of L'?

22 *Problems of Compositionality*

of their constitution properties iff their constituents are synonymous and they have identical syntactic structure.[39]

Using this terminology, the claim that a language conforms to the principle of functionality says that if two complex expressions of a language are indistinguishable in terms of their constitution properties, then they must be also indistinguishable in terms of their meaning properties. The principle of functionality has the form of what Jaegwon Kim calls a *weak supervenience* thesis:[40]

> *Weak Supervenience:* Necessarily, for any property F in Φ, and for any object x, if x has F, then there is a property G in Ψ such that x has G, and if any y has G it has F.
> In symbols: $\Box(\forall F \in \Phi \forall x(Fx \rightarrow \exists G \in \Psi(Gx \wedge \forall y(Gy \rightarrow Fy))))$

The standard name for the members of Φ is 'supervenient properties' and Ψ is called the 'supervenience base'. In the principle of functionality, the supervenient properties are the meaning properties and constitution properties provide the supervenience base. The values of x and y are complex expressions. So, the functionality principle can be stated as follows:

> Necessarily, for any meaning property M and for any complex expression e, if e has M, then there is a constitution property C such that e has C, and if any complex expression e' has C then e' has M.

Take Moore's claim that moral properties supervene on physical ones. According to the weak supervenience scheme this would mean the following: necessarily, whenever you take a moral property, say honesty, then for any person who is honest there is a certain physical property that she has, and whoever else has that exact physical property is also honest. Similarly, the principle of functionality says that necessarily, if you take any meaning property, say having the meaning that Caesar was murdered in March, then for any expression that has

---

[39] * Note that the definition of constitution properties is such that (i) only complex expressions have such properties, and (ii) two different complex expressions can be indistinguishable in terms of their constitution properties even if they contain different (but synonymous) constituents.

[40] Kim (1984), p. 64.

The Principle 23

that exact meaning, there is a certain constitution property that the expression has, and whatever other expression has that constitution property has the same meaning.

In the case of the thesis that the moral supervenes on the physical, 'necessarily' might be taken as quantifying over possible worlds, in the case of the claim that meaning supervenes on constitution, 'necessarily' quantifies over possible human languages. The principle of functionality makes a commitment about which abstract sign-systems could be languages *for us*.[41] This gives us the following reading for the principle of functionality:

> For all possible human languages L, for any meaning property M and for any complex expression e, if e has M in L, then there is a constitution property C such that e has C in L, and if any complex expression e' has C in L then e' has M in L.

Kim argued persuasively that weak supervenience does not capture what we mean by determination. The thesis that moral properties weakly supervene on physical properties demands that there could not be two persons in any possible world who are physically indistinguishable, but have different moral properties. However, weak supervenience of moral properties on physical ones is compatible with the supposition that there is a possible world w that is physically indistinguishable from our world, but where some person who is honest in our world is dishonest. But the existence of such a possible world is incompatible with the claim that one's physical properties determine

---

[41] * The suggested reading for the function principle may seem somewhat counter-intuitive. One might think that the proper way to formulate the principle would have to be relative to particular languages. After all, it seems that whether there are non-synonymous phrases built from synonymous lexical items using the same syntactic steps is a question about English, and has nothing to do with other actual, let alone merely possible human languages. But I think this is not so. The fact (if it is a fact) that there is a such a function in English may have a lot to do with what is going on in other possible human languages. For it may well be the case that the proper *explanation* for why there are no non-synonymous phrases built from synonymous lexical items using the same syntactic steps in English goes like this: The existence of such phrases is logically incompatible with the existence of a function which assigns the meanings of complex expressions to the meanings of their constituents and their structure. However, there is such a function in every possible human language, and since English is one of these, there is one for English as well.

24   *Problems of Compositionality*

one's moral properties. The problem is that weak supervenience requires only that for every property F in Φ there is a base G in Ψ, but it does not say that this G has to be the same in each possible world.

The problem is the same as the one raised by the example of L'. The principle of functionality is not incompatible with the supposition that there are possible human languages which are indistinguishable from an actual language in terms of the constitution-properties of their expressions, but where expressions have different meanings. This means that the principle of functionality does not exclude L' as a possible human language. But the existence of such a possible human language is incompatible with the claim that the meaning of a complex expression is determined by the meanings of its constituents and by its structure.

According to Kim, the strengthening of weak supervenience that we need to approximate the force of what we mean by determination is the following:[42]

> *Strong Supervenience:* Necessarily, for any property F in Φ, and for any object x, if x has F, then there is a property G in Ψ such that x has G, and *necessarily* if any y has G it has F.
> In symbols: $\Box(\forall F \in \Phi \forall x(Fx \rightarrow \exists G \in \Psi(Gx \land \Box \forall y(Gy \rightarrow Fy))))$

(Note that this differs from the weak supervenience thesis only in that it contains a second, embedded occurrence of the necessity operator.)

If moral properties strongly supervene on physical ones, the above cases are ruled out: the physical alter ego of an honest person in a different world is never dishonest. Similarly, if meaning properties strongly supervene on constitution properties, a complex expression constitutionally identical to the English sentence 'Elephants are gray' cannot mean that Julius Caesar was murdered on the ides of March, even if this expression belongs to another possible human language. By applying the strong supervenience scheme to meaning properties and constitution properties and transforming the necessity operators into explicit quantification over possible human languages, we get what I take to be the best paraphrase of the principle of compositionality:

---

[42] Kim (1984), p. 65.

The Principle

25

> For all possible human languages L, for any meaning property M and for any complex expression e, if e has M in L, then there is a constitution property C such that e has C in L, and for any possible human language L' if any complex expression e' in L' has C in L' then e' has M in L'.

To say that L' is not a possible human language is to assert that it is a language that cannot be learned by human beings as a *first language* under normal social conditions. This certainly does not mean that it cannot be learned at all. On the contrary, it is very easy to learn it, once one speaks L. L' is a kind of secret code system that we can acquire on the basis of our antecedent knowledge of another language, upon which it is based. However, if the principle of compositionality is true, we could not learn such a code as our native tongue.[43]

I am not sure whether strong supervenience really captures everything that is meant by determination. However, I am convinced that if the Φ-properties determine the Ψ-properties, then *at least* the latter strongly supervene on the former. The analysis shows what the mistake of confusing the principle of functionality and the principle of compositionality amounts to. It is a certain modal error: the failure to recognize the difference between special instances of the weak and strong supervenience schemes. The conclusion of this section is that the principle of functionality follows from the principle of compositionality, but not the other way around.

6. SUMMARY

In Section 1, I stated a principle, which I called 'the principle of compositionality'. In Section 2, I quoted five other principles that are occasionally given the same title, and then in Sections 3–5, I argued that—with the exception of the first one—even the slightly modified forms presented at the end of Section 2 are not equivalent to the principle I stated. One important question remains: why should we care more for the principle I prefer than for the others? In the next chapter I

---

[43] Strictly speaking, the principle of compositionality only shows that L and L' are not *both* possible human languages. The claim that L' is not a possible human language follows from the additional claim that L is a possible human language. This, in turn, follows from the assumption that L is a rich fragment of English, and that rich sublanguages of actual human languages are possible human languages.

will try to answer this question. I will start with what I take to be a fundamental problem concerning the nature of semantics, and then argue that the principle of compositionality can play a central role in the resolution of the difficulty.

CHAPTER 2

Linguistic Semantics

1. IS SEMANTICS EMPIRICAL?

Linguists who work on semantics tend to think of their discipline as an empirical science, part of a theory about the nature of human languages. According to this view, semantics, like other branches of linguistics, uses primarily judgments of competent speakers about various expressions as data, and attempts to provide systematic explanations of these judgments. Semantic theories are predictive, since they can tell us what the judgments of competent speakers will be in a number of previously unsurveyed cases. The theory formulates hypotheses about natural languages and tests them in the light of semantic intuitions.

Many philosophers are highly suspicious of semantics. It is a remarkably widespread belief among them that semantics, as we know it, is a pseudo-science whose practitioners do not really know what they are talking about. Skepticism about semantics is a lot more fashionable than skepticism about physics, biology, or even psychology.

Philosophical reflection is usually conservative in its perspective on the development of the sciences. Early stages in the history of a scientific theory are often conceptually confused, and philosophers are eager to point out the obscurities. But many philosophers go much further than complaining about unclarities in semantics. They doubt that the difficulties can ever be met. There are two main reasons for this deep skepticism. The first concerns the *methodology* of semantics, the second its *subject matter*.

The methodological worry is that semantic inquiry does not seem to be driven by observation and experiment in the way empirical

27

28   *Problems of Compositionality*

sciences are. Instead, it is often philosophical theses that seem to influence semantics. It is one's views on ontology that determine whether one endorses with the Russell of the *Principles of Mathematics* the semantic thesis that a sentence cannot be meaningful unless there is a certain complex entity, called 'proposition' that is expressed by it. It is one's epistemological convictions that decide whether one agrees with the Kripke of *Naming and Necessity* about the semantic claim that a name cannot refer unless a special causal chain exists between its utterance and a dubbing event in the past. One should be suspicious of the claim that semantics is driven by the linguistic intuitions of competent speakers, given the fact that so many interesting semantic theses were proposed to resolve or create philosophical perplexities. The intuitions that are used in assessing semantic questions are rarely purely linguistic.

The quick reply from the linguist to this allegation would be that the philosophical connections of semantics are not more numerous than those of many other empirical sciences. The search for the right kind of ontology and epistemology can lead thinkers to discoveries in semantics, just the way the search for the *lapis philosophorum* led to discoveries in chemistry. For example, we know that Russell abandoned his early theory of denotation mainly for philosophical reasons.[1] But the reason his theory of descriptions is more popular among semanticists than his early view is (or could be) simply that it copes better with the available evidence. If definite descriptions are phrases "denoting one single definite term by means of a concept"[2], why is the sentence 'The man standing next to me never stops talking' ambiguous? (Note that according to the terminology of the *Principles* 'term' is synonymous with entity, and denoting is roughly the same as what we nowadays call referring. When we use a denoting expression in a sentence, we are making a claim *about* what the expression denotes.[3]) After all, if 'the man standing next to me' denotes a single definite term, the sentence should be straightforwardly true or false depending on what is the case with that term. However, it is a hard empirical fact that the sentence *is* ambiguous. It has a reading according to which there is (exactly) one man standing next to me who is always

---

[1] Cf. Cartwright (1987).

[2] Russell (1903), p. 62.

[3] Cf. Russell (1903), p. 43, p. 45, p. 47, p. 53.

Linguistic Semantics 29

talking, and another according to which it is always the case that there is (exactly) one man standing next to me who is talking.[4] In the second case the man who jabbers can be different at different times. The fact that Russell was led by other considerations in rejecting his original assumptions about the interpretation of descriptions is only of historical interest.

But the quick reply is not completely satisfactory. The judgment concerning the ambiguity of certain sentences containing definite descriptions used against the early Russell's view is indeed straightforwardly linguistic and non-philosophical. Anybody who is a competent speaker of English can appreciate the ambiguity, even if she does not realize it immediately. No special knowledge about the world seems to be required. However, it is not clear that the relevant judgments are always like this.

Consider the question, originally asked by G. E. Moore, whether the sentence 'I don't believe it's raining, but as a matter of fact it is' can be used to make a correct assertion under certain circumstances. (To ask this is not the same thing as to ask whether Moore is right in saying that it is "perfectly absurd or nonsensical to say such thing."[5] Absurd or nonsensical things might still be correctly, albeit falsely, assertible.) It seems to me that there are certain things about the semantics of the verb 'believe' that one cannot say without answering this question. The problem is first, that most of us do not seem to have any firm intuitions here, and second, that one can rightly suspect that if somebody does have strong intuitions, that is because she has a philosophical view to defend. As a consequence, we face a dilemma: either we give up the idea that we can spell out the semantics of a certain word, or we accept that in doing so, we have to rely on intuitions and considerations that are not linguistic in nature.

The problem is quite general. What semantics is supposed to explain is the nature of *linguistic* intuitions ordinary speakers have. However, it is doubtful whether the linguistic and the non-linguistic intuitions can be sorted out from one another. If the line cannot be drawn, semantics is an inseparable part of the systematic reflection on

---

[4] * I put the word 'exactly' in parenthesis because I doubt that the uniqueness implications of definite descriptions are a matter of semantics. This is unimportant here; for details, see chapter 5 and my "Descriptions and Uniqueness."

[5] Moore (1944?), p. 207.

30   *Problems of Compositionality*

the nature and justification of the intuitions and convictions human beings have. And this would mean that there might well be no way to separate the methodology of semantics from that of philosophy.

The other worry about the nature of semantics is connected with the first, but it is more radical. It concerns the subject matter of semantics. What semantics is *about* does not yield itself to any straightforward empirical investigation. Semantics is supposed to be a theory about how and why we can talk about the world. But how could it be that without being a theory *of everything* we can talk about? This is a problem that was raised by Bloomfield, who argued that semantics is not possible, since it presupposes a completed scientific theory of the world:[6]

> The situations which prompt people to utter speech include every object and happening in the universe. In order to give a scientifically accurate definition of meaning for every form of a language, we would have to have a scientifically accurate knowledge of everything in the speaker's world. The actual extent of human knowledge is very small compared to this.

Take the expression 'electron'. It is plausible that a correct semantic theory of English will—among other things—tell us that this word is somehow related to electrons.[7] Of course, if the word 'electron' is related to electrons, then there must *be* such things. Moreover, semantics should say something about what makes it the case that there is such a relation between 'electron' and electrons. But if semantics

---

[6] Bloomfield (1933), p. 139. The passage is quoted in Fodor (1980), p. 248.

[7] Deflationsts may reject this claim. Deflationism in its most radical form is a philosophical theory about the proper interpretation of claims made by the semanticist. For example, according to the *pure disquotationalism* of Field (1994), claims like "Aristotle' refers to Aristotle' and "Snow is white' is true if and only if snow is white', are instances of general principles associated with the semantical terms 'refers to' and 'true'. The examples of semantic claims that one would use to show the non-triviality of semantics, like "Schnee ist weiss' if and only if snow is white', or 'If we had used 'Snow is white' in a different way it would be true if and only if grass is green' are declared to be ambiguous: false under the standard interpretation, but true under some other closely related interpretation. For Field, semantics is certainly not an empirical science. There is nothing to be *discovered* in semantics, since the theorems of a semantic theory express nothing but certain obvious facts about the proper use of expressions like 'refers to' and 'true'.

Linguistic Semantics

31

tells us that there are electrons and what it is for our word to stand in the right relation to them, what is left for physics, or psychology?

One way to reply to Bloomfield's problem is to deny that semantics has anything to do with the relationship between expressions and the world. What a semantic theory does is nothing more than present translation manuals from one language to another, or maybe from one idiolect to another. The theory starts with a dictionary and then extends the translation in some systematic manner from lexical items to complex expressions. The problem with such a reply is that it seems to make a very grave concession. A translation manual does not provide *explanations* for the semantic intuitions of competent speakers: it merely establishes certain connections between intuitions present among users of one language and intuitions present among users of another. To say that speakers of English think the sentence 'The man standing next to me never stops talking' is ambiguous because speakers of Hungarian think that its translation 'A mellettem álló férfi soha nem hagyja abba a beszédet', is ambiguous certainly does not bring us closer to the understanding of the phenomenon.

If a semantic theory is supposed to be anything more than a mere translation manual which defers the specification of the semantic features of expressions from one language to another, it is completely unclear how there could be such a discipline. And even if we assume that these difficulties can be met somehow, it remains clear that the theory cannot be based merely on the empirical data linguists can collect from ordinary speakers of a language.

Both difficulties—the one concerning methodology, and the one concerning subject matter—indicate that semantics as a whole cannot be a straightforward empirical science. In virtue of its methodology, it cannot be completely separated from philosophy; in virtue of its subject matter it cannot be completely separated from psychology.

I think these difficulties are real. What they indicate is that semantics—broadly construed as an account of how and why we can express and communicate our thoughts through a certain language—is not a straightforward empirical enterprise based solely on the intuitions of ordinary speakers. However, it is also clear that semantics, in this broad sense, is not what linguists do. Their subject matter is restricted to some relatively small segment of this vast area, and their methodology is only appropriate as far as the study of that area is concerned. Semantics is not a unitary enterprise: a certain part of it is a

32   *Problems of Compositionality*

purely empirical investigation based on the data collectible from competent speakers, while the rest is a conceptual inquiry connected to everything we know about the world. I will call the former part *linguistic semantics*, and the latter *philosophical semantics*. The separation does not mean that the two branches of semantics are completely independent, only that philosophical considerations do not have an immediate impact on linguistics, and that interesting observations about English or Swahili is unlikely to resolve deep philosophical questions.

In the next two sections I will outline a more or less classical conception of what semantics consists in. Then I will turn to the question how, given this conception of semantics, a significant part of linguistic semantics can be separated from the rest of the theory. The principle of compositionality will turn out to be crucial in making the separation.

2. THE FIRST DOGMA

Expressions have numerous properties that are relevant to the study of language. Some of these concern the way an expression is pronounced or spelled, some concern how it can be combined with other expressions, others how it descended from expressions of other languages. The linguistically relevant properties of expressions can be arranged into clusters, and the members of these clusters determine relations between the expression and other entities. For example, the phonological properties of an expression e determine relations between e and certain sound patterns which are instances of an utterance of e, the syntactic properties of e determine relations between e and larger expressions in which e is a constituent, and the etymological properties of e determine relations between e and other expressions from which e historically evolved. The properties in these clusters—as their names suggest—form the subject matter of the various branches of linguistics.

What underlies the division of linguistics into several branches is the relative independence of the properties belonging to these clusters. The independence is established by certain counterfactuals. English has a word 'ocean' which contains the sound 'sh', is a common noun, and comes from the Greek ''Ωκεαός'. There could have been a word instead of 'ocean' with the same phonological and syntactic properties, but etymologically unrelated to the Greek word. (Whether this other

Linguistic Semantics 33

word would be an expression of English, or of some other possible language English' depends on what the exact identity conditions are for languages. For the sake of simplicity, I will assume that languages are identified by all linguistically relevant properties of all their expressions. Consequently, any change in a language will be regarded as replacing the language with a slightly different new language.) Similarly, there could have been a word with the same syntactic and etymological properties, but pronounced with a 'k', rather than an 'sh', or a word with the same phonological and etymological properties, but which is an adjective, rather than a noun.[8]

Certain properties of an expression concern the way the expression can be significant, the role it plays in a language. Such properties are traditionally called *semantic*. It is a semantic property of an expression that it refers to such-and-such entity, and that it has such-and-such meaning. The semantic properties of expressions are independent of the phonological or etymological properties. There could be a language where there is a word with the same phonological and etymological properties as the word 'ocean', but referring to huge rivers. ('Ὠκεαός, after all, was a river surrounding the Earth, according to the Greeks.) And there could be languages where there is a word which has the same semantic properties as the English 'ocean', but pronounced differently and/or descending from a language other than Greek. Whether semantic properties are also independent of syntactic properties is a much more complicated question.

It is beyond doubt that there are many expressions with the same syntactic properties that are semantically different. But what about the other direction? Could a word mean what 'ocean' does in English without being a common noun? Perhaps we could imagine a language *Venglish* much like English, where the word 'ocean' is a verb. It would contain sentences like 'The Pacific oceans, but the Mediaterranean does not ocean', and 'The stuff which oceans is cold' having the same meaning as our English sentences 'The Pacific is an ocean, but the

---

[8] * As in Chapter 1, I cash the modal force of linguistic principles in terms of quantification over possible human languages. It should be noted, however, that not all linguistic principles quantify over *all* possible human languages. Some are more parochial generalities, where the domain of quantification over possible human languages is tacitly restricted.

34 *Problems of Compositionality*

Mediterranean is not', and 'The ocean is cold', respectively.[9] Of course, these sentences (and the numerous others that one could generate following the pattern) do not establish conclusively the possibility of Venglish. Perhaps Venglish violates some basic organizational principle, and consequently there just cannot be such a human language: the expression that we can use to talk about oceans must be a common noun. Semantic properties form a cluster that may not be entirely independent of the cluster of syntactic properties: the separation between syntax and semantics can only be accepted tentatively.

I described above the phonological, syntactic and etymological properties of an expression as determining relations between the expression and other entities. Traditionally, semantic properties are also viewed in this way. Instead of saying that 'Julius Caesar' has the property of referring to Julius Caesar, we could say that the name stands in a certain relation to Julius Caesar. Similarly, instead of saying that 'Julius Caesar was murdered on the ides of March' has the property of having the meaning that Julius Caesar was murdered on the ides of March, one can say that the sentence stands in a certain relation to *that* Julius Caesar was murdered on the ides of March. I will call the entities that are associated in a semantic theory with the expressions of a language in virtue of their semantic properties *semantic values.*

A semantic theory may assign no semantic value, or many semantic values to certain expressions of a language *L*. It is also possible that expressions have many different types of semantic values. For example a semantic theory can associate with the word 'electron', any or all of the following: a set of electrons, a function from possible worlds to sets of electrons, a function from pairs of possible worlds and time points to sets of electrons, the concept of electron, the meaning of the word 'electron', the mental image of electron, Einstein's conception of electron, recognitional criteria for electrons, the synonym class of the word 'electron', etc.

It is common ground among linguists and philosophers that a semantic theory should include assignment of some kinds of semantic

---

[9] Cf. Quine (1960), pp. 176 - 86, on 'Pegasizing' and 'Socratizing'. The idea that one might shuffle with the syntactic categories of expressions goes back at least to Leibniz: "in place of saying that man is a 'reasonable animal' we could, if language permitted, say that man is an 'animable rational'." Leibniz (1765), p. 292. The question is, of course, whether there could be a human language in which we have such an expression.

Linguistic Semantics 35

values to expressions. However, it is controversial whether all semantic properties should be analyzed in such a way. The thesis that meanings are semantic values amounts to the following:

The First Dogma about Meanings: An expression is meaningful if and only if there is a semantic value m, (called the meaning of the expression) and there is a relation R (called the meaning relation) such that the expression bears R to m.

This dogma was implicitly assumed in the discussion in the previous chapter concerning the relationship between the principle of compositionality and other theses: I talked about meanings and their relations to various expressions. Since I regard this kind of talk as essential to semantic theorizing I will now briefly consider two objections to the first dogma, both of which originate with Quine. They concern the move from accepting properties like *having such-and-such meaning* (I called these in Chapter 1 *meaning properties*) to entities that are *meanings*.

The first argument is based on considerations of theoretical parsimony. Entities should not be multiplied beyond necessity. The only good reason for the belief in the existence of a certain entity is its indispensability in our construction of the best theory, and no reason was given that we really need meanings in semantics.

In the famous ontological debate between McX and WVQ, the former tries to defeat the latter's strict nominalism by arguing that since expressions have meanings, there must be some abstract entities, called meanings, that the expressions are related to. Quine's reply is the following:[10]

> I feel no reluctance toward refusing to admit meanings, for I do not thereby deny that words and statements are meaningful. McX and I may agree to the letter in our classification of linguistic forms into the meaningful and the meaningless, even though McX construes meaningfulness as the *having* (in some sense of 'having') of some abstract entity which he calls a meaning, whereas I do not. I remain free to maintain that the fact that a given linguistic utterance is meaningful (or *significant*, as I prefer to say so as not to invite

---

[10] Quine (1948), p. 11.

36   *Problems of Compositionality*

> hypostasis of meanings as entities) is an ultimate and irreducible
> matter of fact; or, I may undertake to analyze it in terms directly of
> what people do in the presence of the linguistic utterance in question
> and other utterances similar to it.

I think, WVQ is right in pointing out that nothing McX said implies
that meanings have to be abstract entities. However, McX is right about
the innocent claim that there are meanings. I will argue that neither of
the ways of rejecting the existence of meanings mentioned in the last
sentence of the quote is acceptable.

There are two problems with the suggestion that one could take the
meaningfulness of expressions as an ultimate and irreducible fact. First,
it reflects a certain metaphysical bias, according to which postulating
the existence of peculiar entities, like meanings, is problematic, but
accepting the ultimate irreducibility of equally problematic matters of
fact is palatable. It is certainly true that although there are no dragons,
the property of being dragonlike has true applications. But this should
be explained by some story about how that property is related to other,
less problematic properties. It would be strange to say that it is an
ultimate and irreducible matter of fact that some things are dragonlike.
Similarly, if there are no meanings, it is somewhat awkward to say that
being meaningful is something ultimate and irreducible. Second, it
excludes the possibility of any systematic theory about meaning. If it is
an irreducible fact that 'Elephants are gray' is meaningful, and that
'Julius Caesar was murdered on the ides of March' is meaningful, then
there is no prospect for an explanation of why they seem to be
meaningful in radically different ways, and what that difference
consists in. Such explanation requires distinctions among various ways
of being meaningful, and the recognition that the differences depend
on—among other things—the structure of these expressions. This
amounts to the rejection of the idea that the meaningfulness of these
expressions is ultimate and irreducible.

Quine entertains the possibility that the fact that some expressions
are meaningful and others are not might be an ultimate and irreducible
fact only for dialectical reasons. His official answer to McX's challenge
is the second one: that we should analyze the meaningfulness of
expressions in terms of what competent speakers do in the presence of
an utterance in which the expression occurs, and hence, we do not have
to believe in the existence of meanings. The problem with this idea is

Linguistic Semantics 37

twofold. First, the proposed analysis rests on behaviorism, and it inherits all the difficulties that position has. The notion of a behavioral disposition is either understood narrowly, including only perceptible bodily movements, in which case it seems to be insufficient as an explanatory base for the enormous variety of linguistic meanings, or widely, including intentional states and perhaps facts about the environment, and then it ceases to be an intelligible enterprise. If this is the only thing a semanticist can do, Bloomfield's problem is certainly unanswerable. Second, Quine's proposal is not incompatible with the existence of meanings. If the meaningfulness of linguistic expressions could be fully explained in terms of behavioral dispositions, one should say that the meanings of the expressions *are* complex patterns of behavioral dispositions. A reductive analysis does not eliminate the entities, although it may clarify issues of ontology. If entities of type A can be reduced to entities of type B, then in our ultimate ontology we do not have to speak of entities of type A. This is not because there are no such things, but because we do not need separate names for them. (Of course we still may want to keep the names for convenience.) We probably should insist that there are numbers, beliefs, and virtues, even if at some point we become convinced that these can be reduced to other things. It is unlikely that meanings should be different in this regard. Semantics, like mathematics, psychology or moral philosophy, should not be regarded as impossible just because we are unclear about what exactly it is about.

There is, however, a second Quinean argument against meanings. It suggests that they are much more problematic than say, numbers. (Though not necessarily more problematic than beliefs and virtues.) The argument is based on the claim that we have no clear idea about the identity conditions of meanings. If it is indeed the case that we do not know on what grounds we would judge two meanings the same, then it is impossible to regard them as genuine entities.

It is certainly the case that the notion of synonymy is in need of theoretical clarification, and that even after all possible explications it will remain vague. This, however, is true of almost any scientific notion. It would be a more serious problem if it were true that we have no reliable intuitive criteria for synonymy, or if we had strong reasons to believe that there is no way for us to sharpen the initial criteria using theoretical tools. But neither of these seems to me to hold. We make synonymy judgments often, and with great uniformity. There is no

38   *Problems of Compositionality*

question, for example, that 'rich' and 'wealthy' are synonymous,[11] and it is equally clear that 'wealthy' and 'healthy' are not. So, there is an intuitive notion we can start from. We also seem to have certain techniques to sharpen our synonymy judgments. For example, if someone judges two sentences to be synonymous, but is then shown that one of them could be true, while the other was false, she would revise her previous judgment. Furthermore, we see that the reason why many of our intuitions concerning meaning are extremely vague is that we are not used to separating out carefully the pragmatic components of the full information content of our utterances. One might hope that theoretical clarification in this area will contribute to a sharper understanding of synonymy. Quine insists that to accept an appeal to dictionaries and lexicographers in questions of synonymy would be "to put the cart before the horse." This might be true, if one's aim is to reach a notion of synonymy that could ground a set of infallible truths. However, one might safely abandon *that* requirement, and return to what we have, to the ordinary notion of synonymy.

It would be wrong to think that banning the talk of meanings can help to achieve ontological clarity. Whether there are such things among the ultimate furniture of the world should be decided as we go along in presenting a semantical theory, and as we try to incorporate it into a comprehensive world-view. Quine is right in his claim that just because we seem to refer to meanings in our everyday talk, they do not *have to* exist, but—given his commitment to inquiry—he cannot think that our lack of exact understanding of their nature shows that they *do not* exist.

The permissive attitude is, of course, not alien to Quine himself. He agrees that if one resists the temptation to draw immediate ontological consequences from the hypostasis, postulating meanings, or other semantic values is harmless:[12]

> In a longer view, however, this bid for ontological economy is idle. For, once we understand what it is for expressions to mean alike, it is easy and convenient to invoke some special objects arbitrarily and *let* them be meant [...] In choosing a domain of objects for this purpose

---

[11] 'Rich', like most English expressions, has multiple meanings. What I claim is that *one* of its meanings is the same as the meaning of 'wealthy'. Obviously, 'rich' in 'rich food' means something else.

[12] Quine (1978), p. 45.

Linguistic Semantics 39

and assigning them to expressions as their so-called meanings, all that matters is that the same one be assigned always and only to expressions that mean alike. If we can manage this, then we can blithely say thereafter that expressions *have* the *same meaning*. We should merely bear in mind that 'mean alike' comes first, and the so-called meanings are then concocted.

I fully agree with this statement.[13] The starting point certainly has to be a collection of empirical data about which expressions 'mean alike', and which 'mean different'. And the next step is the assignment of appropriate semantic values—meanings—to expressions on the basis of these data.

3. THE SECOND DOGMA

Linguists want to say what the meanings of various expressions are without having to say too much about them. The situation resembles that of the mathematician: she wants to say enough about the number 2 to prove that its square root is irrational, but not so much as to take sides in the metaphysical debate among Platonists, intuitionists and formalists. The aim is to present a set of minimal commitments. The traditional way of doing this in semantics goes via a detour to another semantic value: the referent.

The referent of an expression is a semantic value that corresponds roughly to the Fregean *Bedeutung*. It is linked tightly to how things are in the world, irrespective of how we happen to talk about them. The assignment of referents to expressions is based on two basic theoretical commitments. The first is that genuine sentences are either true or false, but not both. The second is that if they contain a genuine singular term, their truth or falsity depends on the properties of a specific object, picked up by the singular term. The referent of a genuine sentence is its truth-value, and the referent of a genuine singular term is the object it picks out.

These commitments are reasonably clear, except for the repeated occurrences of the adjective 'genuine'. The precaution is necessary: it points to the anomalies of the unqualified versions of these principles.

---

[13] * I did when I wrote this; I am less certain now. The source of uncertainty is the word 'concocted'. Although meanings are human creations, they are not created in the way, say, fictional entities are.

40 *Problems of Compositionality*

We have grammatically well-formed sentences, like Chomsky's 'Colorless green ideas sleep furiously', where people's reactions to the question whether they are true or false will be generally confused. Perhaps such cases can be legislated somehow. But there are others, where all decisions seem arbitrary. How should one assign truth-values to the members of the sequence: 'A man with one hair on his head is bald', 'A man with two hairs on his head is bald', ... , 'A man with one million hairs on his head is bald'? Finally, there are even more troublesome cases, like that of the sentence 'This very sentence is false'. Perhaps, what one should say about some of these expressions is that as far as the semantics is concerned, they do not qualify as genuine sentences.

Similarly, we cannot believe that all singular terms refer to objects. First of all, as we know from Russell, there are problems with descriptions. Then there are names like 'Santa Claus' or 'Madame Bovary'. (We should certainly resist the claim that 'Santa Claus' refers to some benevolent bishop: the truth or falsity of most sentences containing 'Santa Claus' do not depend on the properties of any bishop whatsoever. And Flaubert's remark that he *is* Madame Bovary, should not be taken literally.) The temptation is substantial to say that descriptions and fictional names are not genuine singular terms. This is why the second thesis is also in need of qualification. A semantic theory that assigns referents to expressions eventually has to give some account of what genuine sentences and names are supposed to be, and whence the divergence from sentences and singular terms as syntactic categories.

The simplest and most obvious way to extend the assignment of referents to other types of expressions is to consider them, following Frege, as functors: expressions that turn expressions of a certain semantic category into expressions of another category. The referent of a functor is a function from the kind of entities that are the referents of the input of the functor to the kind of entities that are the referents of the output of the functor. So, the referents of one-place predicates are functions from objects to truth-values, the referents of two-place predicates are functions from pairs of objects to truth-values, the referents of binary sentential connectives are functions from pairs of truth-values to truth-values, etc. Of course, it is an open question whether all expressions of a language can be assigned some appropriate functor-category. It is possible that some expressions belong to more

Linguistic Semantics 41

than one of these, and also that some cannot be categorized at all. In the former case, the expression would receive more than one referent, in the latter it would receive none. In a formal language, like that of first-order logic, these cases are ruled out; in a natural language it is not up to us to decide in advance whether such cases occur.

The meaning of an expression is a semantic value that contributes to the determination of the referent. For example, the meaning of the sentence 'Julius Caesar was murdered on the ides of March' and the facts of Roman history jointly determine that this sentence of English is true. The meaning of the predicate 'unicorn' and certain facts about evolutionary history jointly determine that this word refers to the function that maps every entity to the False. If two people disagree about the truth of the sentence 'Julius Caesar was murdered on the ides of March', but they agree on the fact that Julius Caesar was murdered on the ides of March, they *must* disagree about what the sentence means. Similarly, if someone sincerely claims that she saw something that she calls 'unicorn', while she agrees with the rest of us concerning what sort of animals exist, she *must* mean something else by the word 'unicorn' from the rest of us. It is not entirely clear what sort of modality is involved here, but I am inclined to say that we are speaking of a certain conceptual necessity. This, of course, is not a solution to the problem, merely a labeling of it.

The second dogma about meaning is the following thesis:

The Second Dogma about Meanings: Provided that an expression is meaningful and given the way the world is, its meaning determines its referent.

According to this thesis, the referent of a meaningful expression depends on two factors: facts about the world, and facts about the language to which the expression belongs. Whatever else might be true about the meaning of an expression e, it must be something that is related to the referent of e in this particular way.

Notice that what forces the second dogma on us is that we regard any two genuine sentences that have different truth-values, any two genuine names that refer to different objects, any two one-place predicates that have different extensions, and in general, any two expressions that have different referents as non-synonymous. What this means is that given the way the world is, two meaningful expressions

42   *Problems of Compositionality*

that are distinguishable in terms of their referents must be distinguishable in terms of their meanings. This is equivalent to the second dogma, if one reads it as a strong supervenience claim.[14]

The dogma is occasionally announced without qualifications, as 'meaning determines referent'. I take it that the clause 'given the way the world is' is left out only due to carelessness. However, the omission of the qualification 'provided that an expression is meaningful' is not an accident. Dropping this qualification has the unfortunate consequence that one has to believe that whenever an expression has a referent, it must have a meaning too: if A determines B, A must exist whenever B does.

The claim that expressions that refer are meaningful—although it may be justifiable on theoretical grounds—would move us away somewhat from the ordinary and colloquial sense of the English word 'meaning'. Normally, we do not speak about proper names having a meaning. (Although *some* proper names appear in dictionaries.) The second dogma as I state it leaves open the question whether there are expressions whose referents are exclusively determined by the world without any linguistic contribution.

The second dogma seems to bring the notion of meaning very close to that of Fregean sense (*Sinn*). In fact, as far as commitments made by the first and the second dogma are concerned, meanings *could be* senses. But they do not have to be. Besides fixing the referent, Fregean senses have two other functions. They are ways in which a thinker represents or conceives the referent, and hence, they account for the cognitive value of an expression. And they serve as referents for expressions in oblique contexts. There is no doubt that meanings play a crucial role in any account of understanding and in the semantics of oblique contexts. But the minimal commitments of semantics leave the possibility open that in order to understand an expression we need more or less than a full grasp of its meaning. Similarly, they do not decide whether expressions in oblique contexts refer at all, and if they do, what their referent is.

The claim that given the way the world is meaning *determines* referent does not imply that given the way the world is and given what

---

[14] See Section 5 of Chapter 1, where I argued that determination is at least strong supervenience. One could use an analogous argument here to show that the second dogma is stronger than the claim that provided an expression is meaningful and given the way the world is, its referent is a *function* of its meaning.

Linguistic Semantics 43

an expression means its referent is *determinate*. It is perfectly compatible with the second dogma that some meaningful expressions have no referents, and that some (maybe all) others refer indeterminately. Whether the arguments trying to establish the indeterminacy of reference are sound has no bearing on the truth of the second dogma. The minimal commitments of semantics are neutral about this issue as well.

An objection against the second dogma runs as follows. The problem with the thesis is the vagueness of the phrase 'given the way the world is'. In practice, it is clear enough what the dogma states: 'Julius Caesar was murdered on the ides of March' is true in virtue of what happened in Rome in 44 BC and the meaning of the sentence; 'water' refers to H_2O in virtue of the chemical composition of water and the meaning of the word. Still, a certain skepticism is justified with regard to the possibility of making a distinction between the two kinds of determining factors. Take the sentence about Caesar. Maybe if we really tried to spell out the relevant facts about English, we would eventually get to facts about the Romans, and if we really tried to spell out the facts about the Romans we would end up talking about English as well. Meaning may be radically *holistic*: what determines referent is not the meaning of the expression and facts about the world; rather both are simultaneously determined by the world as a whole.

The reply to this objection is methodological. Our talk about meanings and events in the world is an idealization. We assume that the issue of what certain English expressions mean is largely independent of the issue of what was going on in Rome two thousand years ago. This does not mean that we have to deny that *strictly speaking* they may not be. For example, Leibniz might be right, in which case if anything were different, nothing else could be the same. But even Leibniz acknowledges that something could be different, while everything else remains *almost* the same. In physics, the question is not whether there are really frictionless planes, but whether or not the best form of theory we can think of relies on the abstraction from friction. When we neglect friction, we do not claim that we give a description of a scenario that is strictly speaking correct: only that what we say is close enough to the truth.

Similarly, here the question is whether separating the contribution of linguistic and language-independent facts within the restricted domain of those facts that are relevant in the determination of the

44   *Problems of Compositionality*

referent of a word, or the truth of a sentence, is the right kind of move when one designs a theory about language. And there can hardly be any doubt that it is.[15]

There is a certain tradition within semantic theorizing which accepts the second dogma, but uses it as a weapon against the first. There is a crucial notion which conforms to the second dogma, namely the Fregean notion of sense. Senses—the argument goes—are meanings, or at least those parts of meanings that a semanticist should be primarily concerned with. However, if we adopt this view, we will be forced to give up the thesis that meanings are semantic values, entities that the semantic theory assigns to the expressions of a language. Instead of speaking directly about meanings, we have to theorize about the abilities competent speakers have if they grasp them. Dummett writes:

> The sense of an expression is the mode of presentation of the referent: in saying what the referent is, we have to choose a particular way of saying this, a particular means of determining something as the referent. In a case in which we are concerned to convey, or stipulate, the sense of the expression, we shall choose that means of stating what the referent is which displays the sense: we might here borrow a famous pair of terms from the *Tractatus*, and say that, for Frege, we *say* what the referent of a word is, and thereby *show* what its sense is. [...] It is only in some cases—those where definition is possible— that we can convey the sense of an expression by means of a specification of its reference: in no case can we do so by a direct specification of its sense, i.e. by a pronouncement of the form, 'The sense is ... ' (except where this is completed by 'the same as the sense of X', X being another expression). But to grasp the sense of a word is to master a certain ability to determine the truth-conditions of sentences containing it; and there is no reason to impute an ineffable character to such an ability. Even if we cannot say what a sense is, there is no obstacle to our saying what it is that someone can do when

---

[15] I concede that there are cases when the line between linguistic and non-linguistic contributions to the determination of referent seems almost impossible to draw. Take, for example, sentences that are about another language, or sentences that are about themselves. My claim is only that in most cases no such problem arises. That is, I suggest that the problematic cases should be set aside when we form a conception of what meaning is in *normal* cases.

Linguistic Semantics 45

he grasps that sense; and this is all that we need the notion of sense for.[16]

It is important that to say that the meaning of an expression (or, as Dummett himself would put it, an important *ingredient* of the meaning[17]) is a way of presenting its referent is to say considerably more that what the second dogma states. The extra commitment brings extra difficulties. First, the notion of a way of presenting a truth-value seems to be bizarre. In contrast, there is nothing disturbing in the idea of linguistic facts that contribute to the determination of the truth-value. Second, the status of empty names becomes problematic. The problem is not that one has to say that they are meaningless, but that if meaning is a way of presenting the referent, then non-empty names are meaningful, while empty names are not. Furthermore, one is forced to say that if the bearer of a name ceases to exist, the name loses its meaning, which is definitely in conflict with our use of the word 'meaning'.

Still, I think the idea of a mode of presentation of the referent is attractive. Let us suppose that the difficulties can be met, and also that we have a reasonably clear criterion of identity for these ways of presentation. In this case, I see no reason to reject them as semantic values that can be identified with meanings, or with a certain aspect of meaning. Modes of presentations do not have to be eternal, immutable objects that fill the third realm. However, they should not be regarded as things whose existence depends on their being expressed, or grasped

---

[16] Dummett (1973), p. 227. Evans and McDowell repeat Dummett's point by saying that we do not know how to complete the sentence 'The sense of 'and' is ...' , but we can display the sense of 'and' by stating the following condition: for any two sentences S and S', 'S and S'' is true if and only if S is true and S' is true. Cf. Evans and McDowell (1976), p. xiii, also Evans (1982), p. 26. However, if one thinks that the senses of sentences are sets of possible worlds, one can easily complete the explicit definition: 'The sense of 'and' is the function that maps any two sets of possible worlds onto their intersection'. Of course, I do not claim either that this conception corresponds to the Fregean idea of sense, or that is unproblematic, or that the explicit clause is more informative than the truth scheme itself. The point is only that once one is willing to give a specific conception of sense, the difficulty concerning its explicit statability dissolves. If the point Dummett, Evans and McDowell are making is that we do not (or cannot) have such a definite conception, it seems to be dubious that the situation can be helped by trying to *show* what the senses are.

[17] According to Dummett, sense is the central ingredient of meaning, the others are force and tone. Cf. Dummett (1991), pp. 107 - 40.

46   *Problems of Compositionality*

either, since there are many modes of presenting a referent that have never been and will never be expressed or grasped. Modes of presentation can be conceived analogously to the powers of a chesspiece.[18] There are certain rule-governed powers that no past or future chess piece has. However, the power of a piece, i.e. the rules that determine what *it* can do in a chess game, can only be conceived as something inseparable from the piece itself. Similarly, one can say that a mode of presentation cannot be anything but a mode of presentation *of an object.*[19]

Let me sum up what the commitment to the two dogmas about meaning amounts to. The first dogma states that meanings are certain entities that a semantic theory assigns to expressions of a language. It does not say anything about the nature of meanings. The second dogma states that, if an expression is meaningful, then given how the world is, its meaning is something that determines its referent. This says something about what meanings are, relative to what referents are. If the project of assigning referents to expressions fails, the second dogma is empty: it does not tell us anything about what meanings could be.

I would like to set aside the question whether the project of assigning referents to expressions can succeed. I want to concentrate on Bloomfield's problem, which is that whether or not this can be done, the project is certainly not within the scope of empirical linguistics. The assignment of referents to expressions cannot be done on the basis of data available to the average speaker, hence questions like what does 'electron' refer to are not questions for the linguist. And if the relationship between referents and meanings is as stated in the second dogma, it is unclear how the linguist could ever say what 'electron' means. What kind of thing would determine, once the facts about the world come in, what it is that the word refers to?

4. SEMANTICS WITHOUT EPISTEMOLOGY

A semantic theory presents us with certain relations between expressions of a language and their semantic values. In a certain sense

---

[18] Dummett (1989), p. 312.

[19] The point is analogous to the one made at the end of the previous section: if meanings are patterns of behavioral dispositions, or modes of presentations, then there are such things. If we have reasonably clear criteria for individuating these, then we can regard them as semantic values.

Linguistic Semantics 47

these relations must be epistemological: they underlie our epistemic access to the semantic values themselves. However, linguistic semantics—the component of semantics which is based solely on empirical data obtained from ordinary speakers—should be absolutely free from epistemological commitments: it should not entail that epistemological relations of any sort obtain between speakers, expressions, and their semantic values.

The most straightforward way in which a semantic theory can be committed to a certain epistemological relation is for it to be *definitive* in the assignment of semantic values to expressions. Consider, for example, a semantic theory which assigns at most one referent to each of its expression, and has a theorem of the form (1):

(1) The referent of 'Santa Claus' is whatever stands in the epistemological relation R to 'Santa Claus'.

It is possible that an expression does not have a referent because there is nothing that stands in R to it. But if 'Santa Claus' refers, R must obtain between the name and its referent.

Russell's and Kripke's accounts of proper names can be construed as semantic theories with such clauses. According to Russell, a name refers to whatever the speakers using the name are properly acquainted with; according to Kripke, it refers to whatever stands in the appropriate causal connection with the name. In both cases, if there is nothing that bears the appropriate epistemological relation to a name, then the name fails to refer. Since both insist that at least some expressions do refer, both semantic theories are epistemologically loaded.

Robert Stalnaker, in a recent paper,[20] argues for the separation of epistemological issues from what he calls *descriptive semantics*. Descriptive semantics is the enterprise of associating semantic values with the expressions of a language in a systematic manner. One starts with a wide and abstract characterization of possible semantic theories for a given language and, using empirical data, narrows this down to a single theory. In cases of insufficient information, or indeterminacy, such a specification is not possible, so—as with other areas of empirical research—one has to be content with a certain range of acceptable

---

[20] Stalnaker (1997), p. 535.

48   *Problems of Compositionality*

descriptive theories. A descriptive semantics does not tell us anything about the nature of the relation between words and their semantic values, and hence, it avoids epistemological commitment. The epistemological questions belong to a different theory that Stalnaker calls *foundational semantics*.

Stalnaker's separation of foundational semantics from descriptive semantics is the first step towards distinguishing a purely linguistic component within semantics. The foundational questions are clearly outside the domain of linguistics. It is an issue for linguistic inquiry whether natural kind terms are rigid designators, but it is not a linguistic problem whether the word 'water' refers to water due to acquaintance, causal connection, or magic. The epistemological problems of whether we can refer to entities we are not acquainted with (e.g. persons who are dead, unobserved events in another galaxy), or to objects that are not causally connected with us (e.g. the square root of π, parts of a dissertation that are not yet written) cannot be answered just by looking at the data available to linguists. Hence, theorems of the form (1) cannot belong to a descriptive semantics. The claim can be broken into two parts, (2) and (3), where (2) is a descriptive thesis and (3) is an epistemological claim:

(2) The referent of 'Santa Claus' is σ('Santa Claus');

(3) 'Santa Claus' stands in the epistemological relation R to σ('Santa Claus').

(I am using $\sigma(e)$ as the symbol for the semantic value of e.) I think it is fairly non-controversial that such a separation *can* be made. It is more problematic whether it is the right strategy to separate carefully issues concerning the nature of the relation between expressions and their semantic values from the theory that assigns the semantic values to the expressions.[21] This question, however, can only be decided if one sees what kind of explanations a descriptive semantics can provide.

---

[21] Dummett, for example, would certainly disagree. If we *have to* characterize what an expression means by characterizing what someone can do when he grasps the meaning, the separation is certainly objectionable. Of course, to share Dummett's belief is to give up the idea that any part of semantics that deals with meaning *could be* epistemologically innocent.

Linguistic Semantics 49

5. SEMANTICS WITHOUT ONTOLOGY

A descriptive semantics, insofar as it assigns certain things as referents to certain expressions, is committed to the existence of those things. Linguistics, however, has to leave open the ontological, as well as the epistemological questions. Linguistic semantics has to be an ontologically neutral version of descriptive semantics.

It is not immediately clear how anything worth calling semantics could be ontologically innocent. Suppose that one of the expressions of L is 'Santa Claus', and that the semantic theory T for L entails the theorem (2):

(2) The referent of 'Santa Claus' is σ('Santa Claus').

Given a straightforward quantificational rendering of the definite article in the metalanguage of L, (2) implies that 'Santa Claus' has a referent. Now suppose further that the referent that we assign to 'Santa Claus' is a certain friendly bishop called Nicholas, who distributed gifts on his name day to the children of the poor. Then, it seems, T is committed to the existence of bishops.

However, the last step of this argument is fallacious. For the conclusion to follow, it is not enough that the referent is *in fact* a bishop. What is required is that it be a theorem of T that it is a bishop. If no such theorem follows then one cannot deduce from the claim that σ ('Santa Claus') exists, that it is a bishop. Consequently, T in itself is not committed to the existence of bishops. It is not even committed to the existence of Santa Claus. This brings out the difference between a theory that issues (2) as a theorem, and a theory that yields (4) or (5):

(4) The referent of 'Santa Claus' is Santa Claus;

(5) The referent of 'Santa Claus' is a bishop.

If a semantic theory entails (4), the theory cannot be true unless Santa Claus exists; if it entails (5), it cannot be true unless there is at least one bishop. On the other hand, if it entails only (2), and nothing more about σ('Santa Claus'), then it is only committed to there being something that is the referent of 'Santa Claus', without making it explicit what the semantic value is.

50   *Problems of Compositionality*

Still, (2) is committed to the existence of *something* that is the referent of 'Santa Claus', and even if we do not know what this thing is, this commitment excludes the perfectly reasonable possibility that 'Santa Claus' does not refer to *anything*. So, an ontologically innocent semantics cannot issue theorems like (2) either.

This, however, does not mean that the theory is bound to be vacuous. It could yield theorems of the form (7), without yielding any theorems of the form (6):

(6) The semantic value of e is $\sigma(e)$;

(7) If the semantic values of $e_1, e_2, \ldots, e_n$ are $\sigma(e_1), \sigma(e_2), \ldots, \sigma(e_n)$, then the semantic value of f is $O(\sigma(e_1), \sigma(e_2), \ldots, \sigma(e_n))$;

where O is some semantic operation. For example, our theory may not tell us what $\sigma('\text{Santa Claus}')$ is, or what $\sigma('\text{the father of Santa Claus}')$ is, and it might even remain silent about whether there are such things, but it can still tell us that *if* they exist, there has to be a certain relationship between them. For example, we can have a theorem, like (8):

(8) If the semantic values of 'Santa Claus', and 'father of' are $\sigma('\text{Santa Claus}')$, and $\sigma('\text{father of}')$, then the semantic value of 'father of Santa Claus' is $O(\sigma('\text{Santa Claus}'),\sigma('\text{father of}'))$.

Such a theory might be informative, but it may well be also ontologically innocent. I will call a semantic theory that yields some theorems of the form (7), but no theorem of the form (6) a *hypothetical descriptive semantics*.

Linguistic semantics, I contend, is hypothetical descriptive semantics, which conforms to the minimal commitments mentioned in sections 2 and 3. Of course those general commitments *are* philosophical. According to linguistic semantics there are expressions, there are meanings, and these things are in fact associated somehow. Furthermore, there must be objects in the world that are the referents of genuine singular terms, and genuine sentences must be true or false.[22]

---

[22] George Lakoff talks about *basic realism*, a certain attitude underlying empirical semantics. It amounts to the commitment that the world exists, minds exists, other people

Linguistic Semantics 51

But there are no specific commitments within linguistic semantics about the epistemological and ontological status of electrons, and other things we talk about.

A semantic theory might issue the theorems ''Julius Caesar' refers to Julius Caesar' and ''Julius Caesar was murdered on the ides of March' means that Julius Caesar was murdered on the ides of March'. Another semantic theory, might issue the theorems ''Julius Caesar' refers to Aristotle' and ''Julius Caesar was murdered on the ides of March' means that Aristotle was the teacher of Alexander'. The latter theory is incorrect, but its failure is not a purely linguistic matter. Linguistic semantics is a more abstract enterprise. It entails certain instances of the scheme (7), and thereby it establishes dependencies between semantic values. For example, it might tell us that if certain sentences are true, then certain other sentences are also true, or that if a certain expression has such-and-such meaning, then the meaning of a certain other expression is so-and-so.

The question is whether such a theory can exist without being trivial. It is easy to derive tautological instances, like (9), but these are uninformative.

(9) If the referent of 'apple' is the set of gray elephants, then the referent of 'apple' is the set of gray elephants.

On the other hand, highly informative instances of (7), such as (10), are unlikely to follow from any theory that does not tell us what sort of things are apples and gray elephants, or whether they exist at all.

(10) If the referent of 'apple' is the set of apples, then the referent of 'gray elephant' is the set of gray elephants.

It is clear intuitively, that we want theorems, like (11) or (12):

(11) If the referent of 'apple' is the set of apples and the referent of 'gray' is the set of gray things, then the referent of 'gray apple' is the set of gray apples;

---

exist, meaning exists, and our senses provide reliable reports of the status of the external world. Cf. Lakoff (1988), p. 123.

52   *Problems of Compositionality*

(12) If the referent of 'apple' is the set of elephants and the referent
     of 'gray' is the set of gray things, then the referent of 'gray
     apple' is the set of gray elephants.

How can these desirable instances be characterized? And if we are
supposed to know them to be true, while we suspend judgment about
their antecedents and consequents, in virtue of what can they be
discovered?

6. THE THIRD DOGMA

All but finitely many expressions of human languages are complex.
They have smaller parts that occur in countless other expressions. It is
very natural to think of phrases and sentences as composite entities that
are built up stepwise from words via concatenation, and maybe some
other, more complicated devices. It is less appealing to think of them as
being *built up* from phonemes, although in a sense they are obviously
made of phonemes. The reason is that phonemes have no independent
semantic impact: they do not refer, and they have no meaning. What
makes words important is that they are the smallest semantically
relevant units in languages and that the semantical properties of
complex expressions obviously depend on the semantical properties of
the words that occur in them.[23]

Given the standard conception of reference, the thesis that the
referent of a complex expression is determined by the referents of its
constituents and the way they are combined is true by definition. For
example, if the predicate F refers to a function from objects to truth-
values, and if a refers to an object, the question whether $F(a)$ is true is
settled, once one picks out the function and the object. People who
agree on what the constituent expressions in a complex expression refer
to, and who agree on how they are combined, *must* agree on the referent
of the complex expression as well.[24]

---

[23] I neglect here the complication that some parts of words, like prefixes, and suffixes,
are themselves significant.

[24] The fact that compositionality of referents is true by definition follows from the
particular form of the theory of reference I accepted in section 3. If we accept this
definition, instead of saying that reference-assignment in a certain language is non-
compositional, we have to say that reference-assignment is *impossible*. (In practice,
instead of saying this, we could always revise our assumptions about the language in
question. Perhaps what we thought of as one word is actually, two different words with

Linguistic Semantics 53

Whether compositionality holds for other semantic values, and in particular, whether it holds for meaning, is a much more complicated matter. It is obvious that the meanings of complex expressions depend on the meanings of their simpler constituents, and on the way the complex expression is constructed. Such a dependence is one of the most important features of human languages. Furthermore, there is a strong presumption that if a competent speaker of a language fails to understand a sentence, this *must be* because she is in some sense unfamiliar with the meaning of a certain word in the sentence. This is why in an effort to eliminate misunderstanding, participants of a conversation often engage in discussions about the meanings of certain words, or idiomatic phrases, and almost never about the meaning of whole sentences. It seems to be an important fact about our use of expressions that we do not expect any disagreement concerning the meaning of a whole, once all disagreement about the meanings of the parts are settled. Assuming that two competent speakers of English understand quantification, if they agree about the meaning of 'whale' and 'fish', they *must* agree on the meaning of the sentence 'All whales are fish'.

Such considerations yield some support for the claim that the meanings of complex expressions are determined by the meanings of their constituents and their structure. The support is rather weak though, since no clear connection between meaning and understanding was supposed in our discussion. As I remarked in section 3, understanding an expression may require more or less than knowing what it means.

If, however, the principle of compositionality is true, we can say something about the problem mentioned at the end of the previous section. Two interrelated questions were raised: (i) Which instances of (7) should a linguistic semantics entail? (ii) In virtue of what are those instances supposed to be true?

---

different meanings but the same spelling, perhaps what we thought of as a single syntactic structure masks a hidden structural ambiguity.) If one assigns properties, and not functions from objects to truth-values, as referents for certain one-place predicates, the question whether the principle of compositionality for referents is true becomes substantial.

(7) If the semantic values of $e_1, e_2, \dots , e_n$ are $\sigma(e_1), \sigma(e_2), \dots ,$ $\sigma(e_n)$, then the semantic value of f is $O(\sigma(e_1), \sigma(e_2), \dots , \sigma(e_n))$.

Ideally linguistic semantics would be a theory that entails instances of schema (7) where the semantic value in question is meaning, and f is a complex expression built up exclusively from the expressions e_1, $e_2, \dots , e_n$. Let us call these instances *structural conditionals*. If the principle of compositionality is true, it might be possible to come up with a theory that entails all structural conditionals.

If the principle of compositionality—as it was interpreted in Section 5 of Chapter 1—is true, we can understand how the structural conditionals can be true. Take the complex expression f, whose constituents are $e_1, e_2, \dots , e_n$. Let σ assign meanings to these expressions. It is an instance of the principle of compositionality that $\sigma(f)$ is determined by $\sigma(e_1), \sigma(e_2), \dots , \sigma(e_n)$ and the structure of f, i.e. that there is a law-like connection[25] in *all possible human languages* between $\sigma(f)$ and $\sigma(e_1), \sigma(e_2), \dots , \sigma(e_n)$ constituted by the structure of f. These law-like connections are the fundamental features of human languages that are responsible for the truth of the instances of (7).

If the principle of compositionality is true, linguistic semantics can be an empirical investigation of the law-like connections that make the structural conditionals true.[26] So, in a sense, it is the crucial principle in the attempt to meet Bloomfield's challenge. Because of its importance, one could call the principle of compositionality the third dogma about meanings .

---

[25] What are these law-like connections? There are two possibilities. They are either the regularities described by the instances of (7), or some *abstract law* that underlies these regularities. I will leave this metaphysical question open.

[26] Frawley (1992) uses the term 'linguistic semantics' in a similar way. He writes: "Linguistic semantics is the study of literal meanings that are *grammaticalized* or *encoded* (i.e., reflected in how the grammar of a language structures its sentences." (p. 1) "Linguistic semantics is the study of grammatical meaning – literal, decontextualized meaning that is reflected in the syntactic structure of language." (p. 15) "Linguistic semantics is primarily an *empirical discipline*, inductive, data-driven, and therefore involved with what actually exists, not what in principle must be." (p. 5) This last quote shows where my conception is different: I think linguistic semantics has to be explanatory, and consequently, it has to find law-like connections upon which its generalizations can be based. And wherever we discover law-like connections, we discover what must be the case.

Linguistic Semantics 55

Linguistic semantics, as I conceive it, is a rather thin theory. It is not even committed to the claim that the sentence 'Julius Caesar was murdered on the ides of March' means that Julius Caesar was murdered on the ides of March. What is such a theory committed to? Suppose speakers of English might univocally announce tomorrow that that the sentence means something else, even though its new meaning is not idiomatic. It is not up to the linguist to criticize such change; she must simply change her data. What is important from the perspective of linguistic semantics is this: if such a change takes place tomorrow, and if the syntax of English remains the same, there *must* be some constituent of the sentence that changed its meaning. This much is guaranteed by the principle of compositionality, a fundamental principle of linguistic semantics.

I do not want to claim that linguistic semantics is the only thing linguists working on semantic problems do. Obviously not: lexicography is outside linguistic semantics as I characterized it. My claim is simply that—because of the concerns mentioned in Section 2—an empirical semantic theory that is based on purely linguistic data cannot say too much about the semantic values of words. It is not really surprising that lexicography depends on data from experts in philosophy, geography, zoology, or the history of Mannerist painting. My point is simply that the study of semantic *structures* need not depend on data that do not originate from ordinary speakers of a language.

Hilary Putnam has written the following about what semantics is, and should be about:

> Sometimes it is said that the key problem in semantics is: how do we come to understand a new sentence? I would suggest that this is a far simpler (though not unimportant) problem. How logical words, for example, can be used to build up complex sentences out of simpler ones is easy to describe, at least in principle (of course, natural language analogues of logical words are far less tidy than the logical words of the mathematical logician), and it is easy to say how the truth-conditions, etc., of the complex sentences are related to the truth-conditions of the sentences from which they are derived. This much *is* a matter of finding a structure of recursive rules with a suitable relation to the transformational grammar of the language in question. I would suggest that the question, How do we come to

56   *Problems of Compositionality*

understand a new *word* ? has far more to do with the whole phenomenon of giving definitions and writing dictionaries than the former question. And it is this phenomenon—the phenomenon of writing (and needing) dictionaries—that gives rise to the whole idea of 'semantic theory'.[27]

Putnam might be right about the centrality of lexicography within a complete semantic theory. Linguistic semantics, however, has to focus on the structure of complex expressions, not on the meanings of lexical items. It is the former, not the latter, that can be discovered through an empirical investigation based on the competence of ordinary speakers.

7. SUMMARY

In Section 1, I raised the problem whether semantics, as an empirical science, is possible. In Sections 2 and 3, I outlined a minimal conception of semantics and briefly defended its main commitments. In Sections 4–6, I tried to isolate a certain segment of a general semantic theory which is free of specific epistemological and ontological commitments, and hence, could be based on the semantic intuitions of ordinary speakers. The segment, which I called linguistic semantics, derives certain conditionals which reveal the semantic structure of complex expressions. What underlies the truth of these conditionals is a certain law-like connection between the meanings of complex expressions and the meanings of their constituents. Whether linguistic semantics is possible depends largely on whether such law-like connections exist, that is, whether the principle of compositionality is true.[28] This is the question I will turn to in the remainder of the

---

[27] Putnam (1970), pp. 149 - 50.

[28] One might try to present a kind of transcendental argument for compositionality along the following lines: In order for linguistic semantics to be possible (that is, in order that linguistic semantics is not philosophical semantics), it must be that the principle of compositionality is true. But linguistic semantics is possible, since it is actual. Hence, the principle is true. This argument has two premises, both of which might be true, but certainly nothing that I said here establishes them. First, I argued that if compositionality is true, there might be such a discipline as linguistic semantics, but I did not argue that this is the only way to respond to Bloomfield's problem. Second, I did not show that linguistic semantics is actual. No reason was given why one should accept that the current work in semantics is not fundamentally misguided. I am much more confident that the second premise is true, than that the first is. Thanks to Daniel Stoljar for formulating the transcendental argument, and for pressing me on how my position is related to it.

Linguistic Semantics 57

dissertation. In the next chapter, I will look at the argument that is most frequently used to support the claim that human languages are compositional.

CHAPTER 3

The Argument

1. THE ARGUMENT FROM UNDERSTANDING

Many linguists and philosophers, when asked about their belief in compositionality would give the following quick argument: the meaning of complex expressions must be determined by the meanings of their constituents and the way they are combined, since we—in fact—understand them by understanding their parts and their structure. I will call this the argument from understanding. It is the aim of this chapter to show that this argument is not sound. It has an explicit premise, and two implicit ones; I will try to clarify them in this section.

Frege believed that the senses of complex expressions are compounded from the senses of their parts. According to him, there is a certain isomorphism between the structure of a sentence and the structure of a thought expressed by the sentence, and in general, between the sense of a complex expression and the senses of its constituents. As I noted in Section 3 of Chapter 1, taking senses to be meanings, such a principle is a strengthening of the principle of compositionality. Discussing the proper interpretation of Frege's principle, Dummett makes the following observation:[1]

> To say that the sense of the whole is compounded from the senses of
> the parts is to say, first, that we understand the complex expression as

---

[1] Dummett (1991), pp. 144–5. I will not consider the question whether Dummett is right in his interpretation of Frege's dictum. *Prima facie*, Frege's commitment to the full objectivity of the third realm goes against a reading that analyzes a claim about senses in terms of our ability to grasp them.

60   *Problems of Compositionality*

having the sense it does by understanding its parts and the way they are put together, and, secondly, that we could not grasp that sense without conceiving of it as having just that complexity. The second of these constituent theses is a very strong one. It is, in my view, correct; but it needs a very deep argument to support it, or, indeed, to refute it. The first of the two theses, by contrast, is all but banal and is affirmed, in one form or another, by almost everyone who thinks that a meaning-theory is possible at all: how else are we going to explain how we come to associate those senses which we do with complex expressions of our language (including, as frequently remarked, new ones that we have never heard before)?

The two theses identified by Dummett are closely related. The first is that we *do* understand a complex expression by understanding its constituents and the way the constituents are combined. The second is the first strengthened with the additional clause that we *could not* understand any complex expression in any other way. Both are theses about a certain dependence between understanding a complex expression and understanding its constitution. I will call the first thesis the *modest principle of understanding*, the second the *strong principle of understanding*.

Modest Principle of Understanding: We understand a complex expression by understanding its constituents and the way they are combined.

Strong Principle of Understanding: We understand a complex expression by understanding its constituents and the way they are combined, and we could not understand it in any other way.

Since the preposition 'by' as it is used in these formulations resists any simple and straightforward rephrasing,[2] I will try to explicate the modest and strong principles of understanding by identifying some of their crucial consequences.

Suppose I understand how to operate a camera by understanding the text in its instruction manual. If this is the case, it must be true that I

---

[2] Quine uses the preposition in the same way: "Sentences being limitless in number and words limited, we necessarily understand most sentences *by* construction from antecedently familiar words." Quine (1967), p. 75. (Italics added.)

The Argument 61

understand the text, and that the information in the manual determines how to use the camera. Or suppose I understand what the referee's decision is at a particular moment in a soccer game by understanding his gesture. Then I must have understood his gesture, and the conventional significance of his gesture must have determined what the decision was. Similarly, I suggest, if someone understands a complex expression by understanding its constituents and the way they are combined, then she must understand the constituents and the way they are combined, and what she grasps in understanding these must determine what she grasps when she understands the complex expression. Therefore, (1) and (2) are consequences of the modest principle of understanding.

(1) If someone understands a complex expression, she also understands its constituents and the way they are combined.

(2) What someone grasps in understanding the constituents of a complex expression and the way they are combined determines what she grasps in understanding the expression.

The conjunction of these two theses is weaker than the modest principle of understanding. (1) and (2) do not exclude the possibility that it is a mere coincidence that whenever someone understands a complex expression, she also grasps something that determines the meaning of the complex expression. Obviously, this cannot be the case if the principle of modest understanding is true.

The strong principle requires that the particular way of understanding a complex expression which is asserted by the modest thesis has to be the only one. As Dummett emphasizes, this is not supposed to be an empirical claim about what human beings can do. It is not "merely that our route to a grasp of the whole complex happens to lie through grasping the senses of the components: it is, rather, that what our understanding of the complex consists in is an apprehension of its structure together with a grasp of the senses of the components."[3] That is: understanding the constituents and their combination *is the same as* understanding the complex expression itself. Now, if this is true then the converse of the modest principle must hold as well. If

---

[3] Dummett (1973), p. 152.

62 *Problems of Compositionality*

understanding a complex expression consists in understanding its constituents and its structure, then by understanding the complex expression, one understands its constituents and its structure. This means that the strong principle of understanding has among its consequences not only (1) and (2), but also their converses (3) and (4).

(3) If someone understands the constituents of a complex expression and the way they are combined, she also understands the expression.

(4) What someone grasps in understanding a complex expression determines what she grasps in understanding its constituents and the way they are combined.

To make (1)–(4) more precise, some terminology will be useful. The word 'understand' has a fairly broad sense in English. Besides understanding words and sentences, we can speak about understanding how to operate a camera, a gesture of the referee, what the importance of a discovery is, why a proposal got rejected, personal identity or schizophrenia. To understand is to comprehend something, to perceive the significance or nature of something.

To understand a symbol is a rather special case of understanding. Compare the claim that someone fails to understand the theory of relativity with the claim that someone fails to understand the phrase 'theory of relativity'. In the second case one is inclined to distinguish two possibilities: that the person does not understand the phrase because he lacks the conceptual resources for such an understanding, and that he has these resources, but still fails to understand the phrase because he does not speak English. What it is for an infant not to understand the phrase 'theory of relativity' is radically different from what it is for a Chinese adult not to understand it. No comparable distinction exists in the case of the theory of relativity. You get it, or you don't.

To understand something, is to grasp certain relevant features of it. (This is not intended to be a substantive claim, or analysis. The meaning of 'grasp' is not clearer than the meaning of 'understand'.) For example, to understand how to operate a camera is to grasp some features of the machine that are sufficient for using it. To understand a symbol is more than that. It is to grasp relevant features, and to know

The Argument 63

that those features belong to the symbol. For example, to understand a certain gesture of the referee is to grasp its significance (e.g. that a player has to leave the field), and that the particular gesture (e.g. his holding a red sign while blowing his whistle) has exactly that significance. Similarly, to understand a word is to grasp certain relevant features of that word, and to grasp that those features belong to that word.

One can connect the two principles of understanding with the principle of compositionality. There are two assumptions to be made. First, that the feature of a complex expression that one has to grasp in order to understand the way it is combined from its constituents is the structure of the expression. Second, that the feature of an expression that one has to grasp in order to understand it is the meaning of the expression. (So, understanding an expression is grasping its meaning and recognizing that the meaning belongs to the expression.) If these are true, (2′) and (4′) are equivalent to (2) and (4), respectively.

(2′) The meanings of the constituents of a complex expression and its structure determine the meaning of the expression.

(4′) The meaning of a complex expression determines the meanings of its constituents and its structure.

(2′) is equivalent to the principle of compositionality, so if there are good reasons to believe (i) the claim that what we grasp in understanding how a complex expression is combined from its simpler constituents is its structure, (ii) the claim that what we grasp in understanding an expression is its meaning, and that at least the modest principle of understanding is true, then we have a sound argument for compositionality. Here is the fully explicit form of the argument from understanding:

We understand a complex expression by understanding its constituents and the way they are combined. Therefore, what someone grasps in understanding the constituents of a complex expression and the way they are combined determines what she grasps in understanding the expression. But what we grasp in understanding the constituents are the meanings of the constituents, and what we grasp in understanding the way the constituents are

64   *Problems of Compositionality*

combined is the structure of the complex expression. So, the meaning of the constituents of a complex expression and its structure determine the meaning of the expression, i.e. the principle of compositionality is true.

To say that compositionality is true because we understand complex expressions by understanding their components and the way those components are put together rests on the tacit premises (i) and (ii). I will put (i) aside, and argue in the following section that there are some questions concerning the plausibility of (ii).[4] Then I will turn to the criticism of the explicit premise of the argument.

2. MEANING AND UNDERSTANDING

The claim that understanding an expression is grasping its meaning has the flavor of a truism. However, combined with the second dogma about meaning, we get a highly controversial thesis. The claim is that there is something associated with the expression (Frege called it its 'sense') which can fulfill (at least) two crucial functions: to fix its referent and to be its cognitive value. It has been often remarked that the idea that there could be something that plays both these roles is a nontrivial claim.

Frege believed that the sense of an expression is a mode of presentation of its referent. Consequently, he was committed to the thesis that given the way the world is, sense determines the referent. This provides the first criterion of difference for senses: if two expressions have different referents, they cannot have the same sense. Since (5) is true and (6) is false, these sentences cannot have the same sense.

(5) The Morning Star is the planet Venus.

(6) The Morning Star is the planet Mars.

---

[4] * Note that (ii) does not follow from the minimal constraints put on the notion of meaning in Section 1 of Chapter 1. There I said that the meaning of an expression is a feature or property of the expression in virtue of which it has its role in a language. This leaves it open whether grasp of this feature or property is actually required for understanding.

The Argument

Frege also believed that the sense of an expression is what we grasp in understanding the expression. Senses alone ground our rational cognitive relations to expressions of a language. This is the conviction that underlies the second criterion of difference for senses: if a person can rationally bear different cognitive relations to two expressions, they cannot have the same sense. Since one can rationally believe (7), but not (8), these sentences cannot have the same sense.

(7) The Morning Star is not the planet Venus.

(8) The Morning Star is not the Morning Star.

I will call what determines the referent of an expression, given the way the world is its *referential content*, and what one has to grasp in order to understand the expression its *cognitive content*. According to Frege, the sense of an expression is both its referential and cognitive content. If one believes in the second dogma about meaning—as I argued in the previous chapter, one should—and one accepts the claim that understanding an expression is grasping its meaning, one has to follow Frege in making this identification.

There is a well-known argument against such a move, which derives from (a certain reading of) Putnam.[5] Suppose there is a Twin Earth which is indistinguishable from our planet in almost every regard. The similarity is so overwhelming that only quite sophisticated scientific tests could detect any difference. One of these differences between the two planets consists in the chemical composition of a certain transparent flavorless liquid which fills their rivers and lakes. On Earth, the liquid is H_2O, but on Twin Earth it is something quite complicated, which we shall abbreviate as XYZ. Some of our twins (for example yours and mine) speak a language which sounds exactly like English, which we will call Twin English. (According to Putnam, it is a dialect of English, but we do not have to follow him in this claim. We should probably maintain that dialects of the same language are what they are partly due to some common history.) English and Twin English both have the word 'water' which refers to H_2O, and XYZ, respectively. This difference has certain consequences: if Twin Oscar from Twin Earth would visit us here, he could point to a glass of water,

---

[5] Putnam (1975), esp. pp. 218-27.

66   *Problems of Compositionality*

and say *falsely* 'This is water'. Had Oscar pointed to the same glass and said the same words, his utterance would have been true. Consequently, the referential content of the word 'water' is different in Twin English and English. But both Twin Oscar and Oscar are competent speakers of their respective languages. They are duplicates, (or near duplicates, since the substance that makes up most of Twin Oscar's body is XYZ, not H_2O) so we can assume that their psychological states are exactly the same. What each grasps in understanding 'water' is determined by the psychological state he is in, so the cognitive content of the word is the same in the respective languages they speak. The word 'water' in Oscar's English and the word 'water' in Twin Oscar's Twin English differ in referential content, but not in cognitive content.

There are two replies one can give here that are consistent with the idea that referential and cognitive content are the same. One can say either that the psychological states of competent speakers do not determine the cognitive contents of the expressions they use, or one can reject the claim that Twin Oscar and Oscar are in the same psychological state when they say 'This is water' pointing to a glass of water on Earth. Both amount to the claim that understanding is not merely a matter of what is going on in the heads of speakers. It is not merely that meanings are not in the head; whether someone has grasped a meaning cannot be decided by any theory that restricts itself to internal descriptions of the speaker.

Alternatively, one can abandon the Fregean identification of referential and cognitive content. The important thing to notice about this move is that it rejects a crucial premise of the argument from understanding. As I argued in Section 3 of the previous chapter, the second dogma of meanings is not negotiable: whatever meanings might be, given the way the world is they determine the referent. If one does not have to grasp referential content in order to understand, one does not have to grasp meaning, and hence, the argument from understanding fails.

The conclusion is that due to one of its tacit premises, the argument from understanding can only be used to support the principle of compositionality if one embraces a sufficiently Fregean conception about the nature of meanings. What I will argue in the next two sections is that even if we accept this conception, the argument from understanding remains problematic. The reason is that it is unlikely that either the strong, or the modest principle of understanding is true. So, in

The Argument 67

what follows, I will neglect the doubts concerning the identification of referential and cognitive content, and assume for the sake of argument that they coincide. I will speak about meaning as the feature of the expression that we have to grasp when we understand it.

3. THE STRONG PRINCIPLE OF UNDERSTANDING

I agree with Dummett that the strong principle of understanding is a powerful and interesting thesis, and also that either its full defense or its complete refutation would require a forceful argument. Opponents of the principle will find it hard to give an account of our customary expectations during communication. Why is it the case that when someone fails to understand some complex expression we utter, we are naturally inclined to think that there must be some word whose meaning is not clear to him, or that he has some problem in recognizing the structure of the expression? If he could understand all the parts and the structure without understanding the whole, this expectation would not be well founded. And why is it always a good excuse for not understanding some complex expression that it contains a word whose meaning is unknown to us, or that we are not familiar with a certain rule used in its construction? If we could understand the whole without understanding its structure and its parts, such an excuse might sometimes be unacceptable.

On the other hand, proponents of the strong principle of understanding will have trouble with certain intuitions about how we acquire a language. Why does it sound so absurd to say that one could learn a language just by memorizing a good dictionary and a set of syntactic rules? If in order to understand the whole, we only have to understand its parts and the way they are combined, this should be sufficient. And how is it that occasionally we come to understand the constituents of some familiar complex expression after having used it in an unanalyzed form for years? If one could not understand complex expressions without understanding their parts and their structure, in all these cases we would have to conclude that we did not really understand what the complexes meant before we made the analysis.

Granting the *prima facie* difficulties with either position, I still think one should be inclined to reject the strong principle of understanding. Here is a (not very deep) argument that casts serious doubt on it. Consider a child, Arthur, who does not know much English

68   *Problems of Compositionality*

yet. He understands (among others) the English sentences 'It is raining' and 'This apple is red'. Suppose further that Arthur also knows that the English sentence 'Rain is falling' can be used correctly to make an assertion in exactly the circumstances when 'It is raining' can. (He learned 'It is raining' first, and later he realized that the other sentence can be used when and only when the first can, observing that adults use them interchangeably.[6])One is strongly tempted to think that this much already guarantees that Arthur understands the sentence 'Rain is falling'. Also, it seems clear that what was said does not preclude the possibility that Arthur does not understand the English sentence 'This apple is falling'. (Arthur may have no idea what falling is. Or, he may have some idea, but fail to know what it is for an apple to be falling.) However, according to the strong principle of understanding, this is impossible. If Arthur understands 'Rain is falling', by (1) he must understand 'rain', 'is falling' and the predicational combination. Similarly, if he understands 'This apple is red', he must understand 'This apple', 'is red', and the predicational combination. But then by (3), he must understand 'This apple is falling'.[7]

---

[6] My original example in an earlier draft involved the sentences 'It is snowing' and 'Snow is falling'. George Boolos and Alex Byrne both raised the following objection to the claim that the assertability conditions of these two sentences are the same. Suppose snow started to melt, and began slipping down the roof. Then someone might use the second, but not the first to warn someone else. However, I think that 'Snow is falling' means here something like 'Snow is falling from the roof'. The contextual specification is essential: the remark cannot be understood unless there is a salient roof (or some other high place from which snow could slip down) in the surroundings of the place where the warning was made. This is so, because it is the point of the warning that the person who is warned is supposed to be able to identify the source of the danger. If my analysis is correct 'Snow is falling' is ambiguous. I believe that under one of its readings, it has the same assertability conditions as 'It is snowing', so my argument could go through with the original example. However, the pair 'It is raining' and 'Rain is falling' is cleaner, since the analogous problem does not arise here: one cannot assert correctly that 'Rain is falling' if a bucket of rain water is falling down the roof. Intuitions might differ even with respect to these sentences. Daniel Stoljar suggested, that in a driving rain, when the trajectory of the raindrops is parallel to the surface of the earth 'It is raining' would be true, but 'Rain is falling' would be false. I disagree: the raindrops must have fallen from a cloud, even if towards the end of their fall they move in a peculiar way, so in a driving rain it is still true that rain is falling. If the drops did not come from a cloud, but from some other source, both sentences are false. For examples that do not use weather sentences, see footnote 13.

[7] * If this argument works, then our understanding of complex expressions may be less than completely systematic. According to Evans' *generality constraint*, our understanding of a sentence 'Fa' is the result of two abilities: our understanding of 'a' and our understanding of F; consequently, any subject capable of understanding 'Fa' and 'Gb'

The Argument

There are three ways open for the proponent of the strong principle of understanding to reply to this objection. First, she might bite the bullet and say that Arthur indeed must understand 'This apple is falling', and the intuition that he may not is simply misleading. Second, she might deny that 'is falling' is a constituent of 'Rain is falling' or 'This apple is falling', and thereby block the inference from the understanding of 'Rain is falling' to the understanding of 'is falling', or from the understanding of 'is falling' to the understanding of 'This apple is falling'. Finally, she might claim that by knowing how to use the sentence 'Rain is falling' to make correct assertions, Arthur does not yet know everything that he has to in order to (fully) understand it.

I think the first reply can be convincing only if it is combined with a criticism of the thought experiment. One could say that the example is so unrealistic that it distorts our intuitions. This could be because as a matter of fundamental psychological fact, our learning of new expressions *cannot* be as it is stated in Arthur's case. If this is the case, the example may in fact not show anything. However, the burden of proof is on those who believe in the existence of such a fundamental psychological fact. Those who choose the second reply and reject that 'is falling' is a constituent of 'Rain is falling' or 'This apple is falling' accept an even bigger challenge: they have to prove that contemporary syntactic theory is deeply misguided. Probably most defenders of the strong principle of understanding hold the third reply to be the most promising. But how can we characterize the knowledge Arthur lacks concerning the sentence 'This apple is falling'? To say simply that it is a grasp of the meanings of all constituents would beg the question.

Let us take another example. Suppose we introduce the name 'Pitch Dark' for the deepest point below sea level on the Earth. It is plausible to say that (9) and (10) can be used to make a correct assertion in exactly the same circumstances:

(9) Pitch Dark is in the Pacific.

(10) The deepest point below sea level on the Earth is in the Pacific.

---

must be capable of understanding 'Fb' and 'Ga'. (Cf. Evans (1982), p. 101.) Arthur, however, supposedly understands 'This apple is red' and 'Rain is falling', but fails to understand 'This apple is falling'. So, if I am right about Arthur, the generality constraint should be rejected.

70   *Problems of Compositionality*

Suppose that Bert understands the first sentence and knows that the second has the same assertability conditions as the first. It would be wrong to think that he would thereby understand the second: (11) and (12) have different meanings (the first is false, the second is true), and on the basis of his knowledge described above, Bert cannot appreciate this difference.[8]

(11)   It is possible that Pitch Dark is not in the Pacific.

(12)   It is possible that the deepest point below sea level on the Earth is not in the Pacific.

As Dummett puts it: the *assertoric content* of 'Pitch Dark is in the Pacific' and 'The deepest point below sea level on the Earth is in the Pacific' are the same, but their *ingredient senses* are different.[9]

So, in order to justify the claim that Arthur may not understand the sentence 'This apple is falling', despite his ability to use it to make correct assertions, one would have to show by means of a certain embedding that the ingredient sense of 'Rain is falling' is different from that of 'It is raining'. However, it is hard to see what sort of embeddings could be used for this purpose. Modal operators will not do the job, since necessarily it is raining if and only if rain is falling. One might try to construct a case where a person, say Chloe, would have strange beliefs and as consequence of this, (13) would be false, while (14) would be true:

(13)   Chloe believes that rain is falling.

(14)   Chloe believes that it is raining.

---

[8] All this depends on the assumption that Kripke is right in his intuition that all names, hence even those that are introduced by explicit definition, are rigid designators.

[9] "Someone who is able, for a given sentence, to classify specifications of possible states of affairs into those that are adequate for an assertion made uttering it, as a complete sentence, on any given occasion, and then to classify the adequate ones into those that render it correct and those that render it incorrect, may be said to know the assertoric content of the sentence. It does not at all follow that he knows enough to determine its contribution to the assertoric content of complex sentences of which it is a subsentence. What one has to know to know that may be called its ingredient sense, and that may involve much more that its assertoric content. Ingredient sense is what semantic theories are concerned to explain." Dummett (1991), p. 48.

The Argument 71

But could this really happen? It seems impossible to describe the case without begging the question. It is certainly possible that Chloe would assent to 'It is raining', but not to 'Rain is falling', she might even say 'I believe that it is raining, but I don't believe that rain is falling.' However, this does not mean that her assent is correct, or that she said something true when she reported her own beliefs. It is highly unlikely that a competent speaker would ever be in Chloe's situation and the reports of non-competent speakers can be misleading in assessing their beliefs. The problem is essentially the same for other propositional attitude verbs. It does not seem plausible that 'Chloe *V*s that rain is falling' and 'Chloe *V*s that it is raining' can differ in truth value for any psychological verb *V*.[10]

One might try embeddings of a different kind. For example, the following two sentences can be contrasted:

(15) That rain is falling and rain is wet entails that something wet is falling.

(16) That it is raining and rain is wet entails that something wet is falling.

One might argue that under a certain interpretation of 'entails' the first, but not the second of these sentences is true. But what is this interpretation? One could say that under the relevant interpretation of 'entails' if *p* entails *q* then this is solely in virtue of the structure of *p* and *q*, not the meaning of their constituents. Unfortunately, under this interpretation both (15) and (16) are false: if the word 'and' meant something else, the antecedent could be true while the consequent is false. One might try then (17) and (18):

(17) That rain is falling entails that something is falling.

---

[10] One might suggest that double embeddings can be used to distinguish the ingredient senses of 'It is raining' and 'Rain is falling'. Even if it is a fact that believing that it is raining is just the same as believing that rain is falling, Desiré might not know that this is a fact, and then he could wonder whether Chloe believes that rain is falling, while having no doubt that Chloe believes that it is raining. However, I do not think that this case is essentially different from the previous one. I think that the sentence 'Desiré believes that Chloe believes that it is raining but Desiré does not believe that Chloe believes that rain is falling' is false, unless Desiré actually has inconsistent beliefs. Thanks to Dick Cartwright for pressing me at this point. Those who find my view incredible should consult footnote 12.

72   *Problems of Compositionality*

(18) That it is raining entails that something falling.

But if one accepts that (17) is true under the intended interpretation of 'entails', one might also accept that (18) is true. The opponent of the strong principle of understanding can reject the suggestion that the structure of 'Rain is falling' licenses any inferences that one cannot get from 'It is raining'.[11,12]

I would not venture to say that there are no embeddings that show convincingly that 'Rain is falling' and 'It is raining' have different ingredient senses. However, if there are such embeddings, I certainly do not know how to find them.[13]

If one is convinced by this and other examples[14] that the strong principle of understanding is too strong, one might wonder what is

---

[11] The distinction between structurally and non-structurally valid inferences is problematic in general. Cf. Evans (1976).

[12] * I suspect that there will be many readers who are not convinced by my arguments. So, let's suppose that I am wrong and 'It is raining' and 'Rain is falling' actually embed differently. Still, to conclude from this that they have different ingredient senses would be too hasty. If the notion of ingredient sense is of any use, it surely cannot involve *absolutely every* embedding. The difference in truth value between (a) and (b) does not show that the ingredient senses of 'It is raining' and "Rain is falling' differ:
(a)   Eric said that it is raining using these very words.
(b)   Eric said that rain is falling using these very words.
The obvious thing to say is that these sentences make explicit reference to the particular words within 'It is raining' and 'Rain is falling', so the truth values of (a) and (b) depend on features of these expressions that are not part of their ingredient senses. But if this is acceptable here, why not in the cases of (13)/(14) and (17)/(18)?

[13] It is not enough for the argument that one finds two sentences that are synonymous, but have different structure; it is essential that the two sentences belong to the *same* language. Arthur's case is not analogous to that of Felix who does not speak Hungarian, but who learns that the English sentence 'It is snowing' (which she understands) can be used to make a correct assertion in exactly the same circumstances as the Hungarian sentence 'Hull a hó'. This child certainly does not understand the Hungarian sentence, but this fact can be easily accounted for using the distinction between assertoric content and ingredient sense. For example, 'It is not the case that hull a hó' is not a sentence in any language, so—unlike 'It is not the case that it is snowing'—it cannot be used to make a correct assertion at all.

[14] Here are two other examples: Arthur understands 'This boy moved with the pawn' and 'This boy is smart', and knows that the first sentence can be asserted iff 'This boy made a move with the pawn' can. Still, he may not understand 'This move is smart'. Arthur understands 'The boy ran in the park' and 'The train passed slowly', and knows that the first sentence can be asserted iff 'This boy ran for some time in the park' can. Still, he may not understand 'The time passed slowly'. These examples, like the one used in the main text are imperfect: one might contend that the assertability conditions are not exactly the same. However, even if I failed to come up with sentences that have different

The Argument 73

responsible for its falsity. Many would take it as obvious that the problem must be that the principle implies (3). (1), the other consequence of the strong principle of understanding used in the demonstration that Arthur must understand 'Rain is falling', follows from the modest principle as well, and that enjoys a widespread reputation for being trivially true. In other words, most opponents of the strong principle would agree with the last sentence of the quote from Dummett at the beginning of this chapter. Dummett's (and probably many others'[15]) reason for believing that the modest principle must be trivial is the claim that without it we could not explain the fact that we can understand expressions we have never heard before. In the next section I will try to reconstruct an argument along these lines.

4. THE MODEST PRINCIPLE OF UNDERSTANDING

The argument for the modest principle of understanding that Dummett alludes to can be found in Frege's writings. In a letter to Jourdain, he defends the indispensability of sense as follows:[16]

> The possibility of our understanding [sentences] which we have never heard before rests evidently on this, that we can construct the sense of a [sentence] out of parts that correspond to words. If we find the same word in two [sentences], [...] then we also recognize something common to the corresponding thoughts, something corresponding to this word. Without this, language in the proper sense would be impossible. We could indeed adopt the convention that certain signs were to express certain thoughts, like railway signals ('The track is clear'); but in this way we would always be restricted to a very narrow area, and we could not form a completely new [sentence], one

---

structure and are truly synonymous, I hope I succeeded at least in casting doubt on the claim that there *could* not be such sentences.

[15] Steven Schiffer is a notable exception. He is a devoted opponent of compositional semantics who thinks that the argument based on the fact that we are capable of understanding a huge number of expressions we never heard before is fallacious. Nevertheless, he believes that it is "a platitude that one's knowledge of the meaning of a sentence is determined by one's knowledge of the meanings of its words and syntactic construction." Schiffer (1987), p. 214. I agree with the first claim, but not with the second.

[16] Frege (1914?), p. 79. I have replaced the word 'proposition' in the translation by the more appropriate 'sentence'. The German 'Satz' means both, but Frege obviously meant the second here.

74   *Problems of Compositionality*

which would be understood by another person even though no special
convention had been adopted beforehand for this case.

Frege emphasizes that a language that lacks compositional meaning
assignment would be severely restricted in its scope; it could not serve
rich communicative purposes, so in a sense, it would not be a possible
human language. Since it focuses on the fact that we can understand
expressions we have never heard before, I will call it the *argument from
novelty*.

Let me go through my terminology again. The standard argument
for compositionality is the argument from understanding: meaning in
human languages is compositional because we understand a complex
expression by understanding its constituents and its structure. I called
the crucial (and only explicit) premise of the argument the modest
principle of understanding. The standard argument for this principle is
the argument from novelty: it must be true, otherwise we could not
understand new expressions without explicit new conventions.

The argument from novelty has been used, repeated, rephrased, or
alluded to very frequently in the literature. It is part of the semantic
folklore, and it is virtually the only argument ever made in favor of the
modest principle of understanding. The argument certainly sounds
convincing, but when one tries to explore its implicit premises, one
realizes that it is not entirely clear how it is supposed to go. I think it is
reasonable to say that the argument from novelty is an inference to the
best explanation, roughly along the following lines. It is genuinely
surprising that there seem to be a huge (probably infinite) number of
expressions in any human language that its speakers can understand
despite the severe limitation of human cognitive capacities in virtually
all other respects. Our mastery of a language is a grand, maybe infinite
aptitude, despite the fact that we are restricted finite beings. The best
(or maybe the only conceivable) way to explain this is by assuming that
we are familiar with the meanings of a relatively small stock of simple
expressions and with the syntax of the language, and that the meaning
of all other expressions is determined by these factors.

The argument shares all the problems that other inferences to the
best explanation have (e.g. it assumes that there is an explanation to be
found), and it has some of its own. When we use inferences to the best
explanation, we can base our judgment on some sort of authority. In
ordinary circumstances, it is the authority of common sense which

The Argument 75

gives support to the claim that a given explanation is the best. In many scientific cases, it is the authority of a long and established tradition. But there have not been many attempts to explain our ability to understand language. Most people never thought that the fact that they can understand expressions they have never heard before was something to explain, and they would have a hard time appreciating the explanation provided by the modest principle of understanding. It is true that most people would not think that the fact that bodies usually fall towards the earth is something to explain, but—and this is an important difference—they probably do (or would) appreciate that the explanation given by the Newtonian theory of gravitation covers other seemingly unrelated phenomena, like the tides and the movement of the planets. Part of what makes something a good explanation is its comprehensiveness. The problem with the modest principle of understanding is that it explains little, if anything, besides our ability to understand new expressions. One might hope that were we to have a more comprehensive knowledge of the workings of the human mind, the principle would play a crucial role in that theory, but at this point we have no evidence that it is anything more than an *ad hoc* solution to a single problem.

But can we not appeal to common sense, instead of explanatory diversity in supporting the judgment that the modest principle of understanding provides the best explanation in the case at hand? Is the explanation not analogous to ordinary cases when we infer from a particular noise that there is a dog under the window, or when we come to believe by looking at a clock that it is six o'clock? I think the answer is 'no'. In ordinary cases, our judgment is supported by experience and a good grasp of the relevant features of the world. Thinking about how little is known about the actual process of language understanding, I am tempted to say this: perhaps Frege's explanation is the best that we can think of, but it may very well not be good enough. I suggest that most of the intuitive appeal of the modest principle of understanding is illusory, and it comes from the difficulty of imagining what it would be like for it to be false. To bolster the imagination, I would like to present two simple examples.

76   *Problems of Compositionality*

First, consider our ability to understand the Algebraic notation for chess games.[17] Suppose someone knows how to play chess, and also the following things about the Algebraic notation. The rows of the chess board are represented by the numerals **1, 2, ..., 8**; the columns are represented by the letters **a, b, ..., h**. The squares are identified by column and row; for example **e4** is in the fifth column and in the fourth row. The signs for the pieces are the following: **K** for king, **Q** for queen, **R** for rook, **B** for bishop, and **N** for knight. Each move is represented by the capital letter standing for the piece moved and the sign standing for the square of its arrival. If the move is made by a pawn, it is represented only by the sign standing for the square of arrival. If more than one piece of the same type could arrive at the same square, the sign for the square of departure is placed in front of the sign for the square of arrival. If the move results in a capture, x is placed in front of the sign for the square of arrival. The symbol 0–0 represents castling on the king's side, while the symbol 0–0–0 represents castling on the queen's side. + stands for check, and ++ for mate. This much information about the notation enables one to follow the description of any game.[18] One who understands the notation must be able to tell upon reading a description of a game which move is made by which player at which point.

Suppose we have a description of a particular game in the Algebraic notation. The description is a sequence of symbols, representing the consecutive moves made by the players. Somewhere in the middle of the description is the sign **Nf7**. The question is whether we can understand this complex symbol by understanding its constituents and the way they are combined. The answer seems to be negative, since without additional information from the previous lines of the description of the game, one cannot even know what the move **Nf7** is. It must be a move that is made by a knight to the square at the intersection of the sixth column and the seventh row. But the symbol leaves it unspecified exactly which knight made the move, and exactly which square was the place of departure. All this can be determined if one follows the description from the initial position of the pieces step

---

[17] The Algebraic notation is the standard system for describing chess games. Its essentials were invented in the 9th century by the Arabs.

[18] The Algebraic notation also contains additional symbols that are used to express the commentator's opinions about the move. These are inessential for the understanding of the notation.

The Argument 77

by step. What **N**, **f**, and **7** mean, and the way these symbols are combined in **Nf7** play a significant role in our understanding **Nf7**, but they are not sufficient. Something that might be called a suitable *sensitivity to surroundings*[19] also contributes to our capacity to comprehend what this complex symbol means within the description of the game.

One might claim that our understanding of less artificial notations is similar.[20] We rely on our sensitivity to the surroundings whenever we understand a complex expression. This yields an alternative explanation for our capacity to understand new expressions. The explanation goes as follows: we understand complex expressions by understanding their constituents, their structure, *and* by using our general sensitivity to the surroundings of the utterance. This latter factor is constitutive of what it is to be a competent speaker: one among the many things children acquire in learning their native tongue is a linguistic sensitivity to their surroundings. Whether this is a better explanation than the one provided by the modest principle of understanding depends on further details.

As a second example, consider our ability to understand number expressions in decimal notation. The language we will consider generates the number expressions and assigns to each of them a particular denotation. The language, N, has the numerals from **0** to **9** as its atomic expressions. The only syntactic rule is that an atomic expression can be written in front of any expression. So the syntax writes number expressions from right to left. According to the semantics, the domain of interpretation is the set of natural numbers and the atomic expressions are assigned their usual denotations. The interpretation function f will read left to right: if α is an atomic expression and ε is an expression, $f(\varepsilon\alpha)=10f(\varepsilon)+f(\alpha)$.[21] Here is a slightly more systematic presentation of this language:

---

[19] The expression is due to Charles Travis, who uses it in a related context. Cf. Travis (1994), p. 176.

[20] I will argue in Chapter 5 that the behavior of certain definite descriptions in natural languages is in some sense analogous to the behavior of the letter **N** in **Nf7**.

[21] For the sake of simplicity I describe a language that generates the numerals in decimal notation, possibly prefixed by an arbitrary number of **0**s. Janssen (1983) and Zadrozny (1994) discuss this example in a related context.

78   *Problems of Compositionality*

$N= \langle Syntax, Semantics \rangle$

Syntax:	*Semantics*:
0, 1, ... , **9** are atomic expressions,	$f(\mathbf{0})=0, f(\mathbf{1})=1, \ldots , f(\mathbf{9})=9,$
for every atomic expression α and	if α is an atomic expression and
every expression ε	ε is an arbitrary expression,
$\alpha\varepsilon$ is an expression	$f(\varepsilon\alpha)=10f(\varepsilon)+f(\alpha)$

N is a language that does not have a semantics parallel to its syntax. This is not a problem from a formal point of view: it is easy to prove that all the expressions that are generated by the syntax of N receive a unique denotation through its semantics. Let us assume that our understanding of the expressions of N 'follows' its semantics, rather than its syntax. Suppose that we understand the expressions of this language by the following decomposition: faced with a complex number expression ε, we first separate its leftmost digit, and call that the first expression. We use a semantic rule to understand the first expression. Then we separate the next digit of ε from the left and we adjoin it to the first expression from the right, and so we get the second expression. We apply a semantic rule to understand this expression. Then we separate the next digit of ε from the left and we adjoin it to the second expression ..., and so on until there are no more digits of ε to remove.

If this is how we proceed, we have to conclude that N violates the modest principle of understanding: we do not understand its expressions by understanding the constituents and their syntactic composition. Here is why: take the expression **372**. Its syntactic constituents are **2, 7, 72,** and **3**. If our understanding of **372** were in conformity with the modest principle, we would have to understand all the syntactic constituents of this expressions in order to understand it. However, according to our assumptions, our understanding 'follows' the semantic rules of N. Consequently, the smaller expressions we have to understand in order to understand **372** are **3, 7, 37,** and **2**. This list does not contain one of the syntactic constituents of **372**, namely **72**.

One could get rid of the violation of the modest principle of understanding, by bringing the syntax and the semantics of the

The Argument 79

language into harmony. The first way to do this would be to change the syntax. The new syntax will write left to right, i.e. its only syntactic rule is that an atomic expression can be written after any expression:

$N' = \langle Syntax', Semantics \rangle$

Syntax':	*Semantics*:
0, 1, ... , 9 are atomic expressions,	$f(\mathbf{0})=0, f(\mathbf{1})=1, \ldots , f(\mathbf{9})=9,$
for every atomic expression α and	if α is an atomic expression and
every expression ε	ε is an arbitrary expression,
$\varepsilon\alpha$ is an expression	$f(\varepsilon\alpha)=10f(\varepsilon)+f(\alpha)$

Syntax' generates the same expressions as *Syntax*, and these expressions are interpreted in N' in the same way, as in N. One can think of the process of changing the syntax as choosing a more appropriate syntax for the semantics of N. Expressions generated by such more 'fitting' syntactic rules are often called logical forms. Note, however, that this syntax is 'less natural' than the original one: it conflicts with one's pretheoretic syntactic intuitions to say that thirty-seven is a constituent of three-hundred-seventy-two.

The other possibility is to change the semantics, so that it could read number expressions the way syntax writes them: right to left. This is not impossible, but it is much more convoluted than the original semantics. First, we can define recursively the function l that assigns the length of a number in decimal notation to the corresponding numeral. Second, using l, the interpretation function f' can be defined as follows:

$N'' = \langle Syntax, Semantics'' \rangle$

Syntax:	*Semantics''*:
0, 1, ... , 9 are atomic expressions,	$f''(\mathbf{0})=0, f''(\mathbf{1})=1, \ldots , f''(\mathbf{9})=9,$
for every atomic expression α and	if α is an atomic expression and
every expression ε	ε is an arbitrary expression,
$\alpha\varepsilon$ is an expression	$f''(\alpha\varepsilon)=f''(\alpha)\cdot 10^{l(f''(\varepsilon))}+ f''(\varepsilon)$

80   *Problems of Compositionality*

Semantics" is less elegant than *Semantics*, which may suggest that the 'natural' way to assign denotations to number expressions is from the right to left, and not the other way around. And if this is the simpler way to assign denotations, it might be the simpler way to understand the expressions.[22]

The conclusion is that in the case of number expressions, there is some *prima facie* evidence that the syntax and the semantics may not be in harmony. The structure that we seem to grasp when we understand the expressions may be different from their syntactic structure. However, there is something even more important that the example suggests. There may be a single syntactic structure in a language, and still, the understanding of the language may utilize some other structure. Furthermore, there may be many alternative ways to understand the same expression, even if the expression has a single well-defined structure.

Neither the example of chess notation, nor that of the decimal notation is supposed to be conclusive: I presented them merely to shake the conviction that the modest principle of understanding cannot be false. The examples reveal certain theoretical possibilities that were neglected in the argument from novelty. My conclusion is that the argument is not convincing: explaining the fact that we are capable of understanding expressions we have never heard before by using the modest principle of understanding may not be best.

Since the argument from novelty was the support for the main premise of the argument from understanding, I believe that the latter is also in trouble. The standard reasons for believing in the principle of compositionality are weak. This, however, does not mean that these reasons are completely misguided. In the next section I will try to show what *does* follow from the self-evident truth that we can understand expressions we have never heard before.

---

[22] George Boolos has suggested to me a different, and slightly more elegant way to present a semantics for the decimal notation that reads right to left. Let the function f^* be defined as follows: $f^*(0) = \langle 0, 10 \rangle, f^*(1) = \langle 1, 10 \rangle, \dots , f^*(9) = \langle 9, 10 \rangle$; if α is an atomic expression and ε is an arbitrary expression, $f^*(\alpha\varepsilon) = \langle f_1^*(\alpha) \cdot f_2^*(\varepsilon) + f_1^*(\varepsilon), 10 \cdot f_1^*(\varepsilon) \rangle$, where the indices '$_1$' and '$_2$' indicate the first and the second component of the ordered pair, respectively. For all expressions ε of N'', we have $f_1^*(\varepsilon) = f''(\varepsilon)$.

The Argument   *81*

5. UNDERSTANDING AND THE MISSING SHADE OF BLUE

What is so puzzling about the fact that we can understand expressions
we have never heard before? It is often suggested that the difficulty is
that there are too many of these new expressions. Natural languages
contain certain iterative devices, like the connective 'and', and the
expression 'I dreamt'. After a couple of iterations the resulting
sentences become exceedingly complicated and difficult to parse, but
there is no sound theoretical reason to assume that they will be
ungrammatical, or incomprehensible. We should be able to grasp their
meaning, at least in principle.[23]

In 1965 Donald Davidson wrote the following passage, which
underlines the importance of the infinite nature of human languages in
theorizing about their semantics:

> When we can regard the meaning of each sentence as a function of a
> finite number of features of the sentence, we have an insight not only
> into what there is to be learned; we also understand how an infinite
> aptitude can be encompassed by finite accomplishments. For suppose
> that a language lacks this feature; then no matter how many sentences
> a would-be speaker learns to produce and understand, there will
> remain others whose meanings are not given by the rules already
> mastered.[24]

In 1970, the emphasis changes slightly. Davidson still insists that
human languages contain infinitely many meaningful expressions, but
he also argues that this is not the main reason why we should believe in
the compositionality of meaning:

---

[23] This point is almost universally accepted. For a dissenting opinion see Ziff (1974).
Sometimes number expressions are used to argue for the infinity of expressions in a
natural language. Cf. Martin (1994), p. 7. This might seem to have the advantage that one
can avoid explicit iterative devices, but in fact it does not. One can say that English
contains the sentences: 'I have one kumquat', 'I have two kumquats', 'I have three
kumquats', ... , but it is clear that—contrary to what Martin says—one could not
continue this series without recourse to some notation from mathematics. English simply
does not have a standard name for the number 2^{100}. We could, in principle, continue *ad
infinitum* the series 'I have one kumquat', 'I have one kumquat, and I have another one',
'I have one kumquat, and I have another one, and I have another one', ... , but here we
are using iteration on 'and'.
[24] Davidson (1965), p. 8.

82   *Problems of Compositionality*

Since there seems to be no clear limit to the number of meaningful
expressions, a workable theory must account for the meaning of each
expression on the basis of the patterned exhibition of a finite number
of features. Even if there were a practical constraint on the length of
the sentences a person can send and receive with understanding, a
satisfactory semantics needs to explain the contribution of repeatable
features to the meaning of sentences in which they occur.[25]

What lies at the bottom of the idea that our ability to understand new
sentences would be impossible if we did not understand them by
understanding their parts and their structure is the systematicity of this
understanding. If someone is a competent speaker of English, it is
predictable that she will understand the expressions addressed to her,
provided that they are built up in a simple way from lexical items
whose meanings are not too far-fetched. Even if languages were finite,
we would have to account for this.

Do we have abilities that are similarly systematic? I am presented
with an apple that I never saw before, and I know immediately what it
will taste like. But this analogy is far from being perfect: I have tasted
many apples, and I know that they all taste the *same*, or at least that the
differences are too small to be relevant for my present purposes. The
strange thing about understanding new expressions is that they can
mean something *different* from any expression I have ever understood.
Suppose I am told in advance that the apple I will be shown tastes like
no other apple I tasted before. In this case I would refrain from judging
what it tastes like when I am presented with it. However, if I am told
that I will hear an English sentence whose meaning I never grasped
before, this does not give me any reason to doubt that I will
nevertheless be able to grasp it upon hearing it. So, part of what is
remarkable about the phenomenon is that we can grasp *new meanings*
upon hearing new expressions.[26]

Let us then try this: I am presented with the strangely flavored new
apple, I taste it, and I immediately know what it tastes like. Why is this

---

[25] Davidson (1970), p. 55.

[26] Suppose I am a speaker of a peculiar language, where all words that have more than
ten letters mean the same as the English word 'fire'. (Speakers of this language use
different words in order to achieve different stylistic effects.) In this case, there would be
nothing remarkable about my ability to understand infinitely many different words in this
language.

The Argument

not analogous to the case when I am understanding a new expression? Because in tasting the apple, I experienced what it tastes like. However, we do not receive the meanings of new expressions from the expressions themselves when we hear them. I *learned* what the taste of the apple was when I tasted it. But if I am asked whether I learned what the meaning of the expression was upon hearing it, the answer will be clearly 'no'. So, interestingly, the other remarkable fact about understanding new expressions is that what we grasp when we hear them are in some sense *familiar meanings*.[27]

Let me put this paradoxically: we understand new expressions with new meanings, but we understand them without learning anything new, so—in another sense—the meanings must be familiar. An analogous phenomenon puzzled Hume in the *Treatise* and in the first *Enquiry*. After arguing for the strong empiricist thesis that all our ideas originate from impressions, he mentions a 'contradictory phenomenon':

> Suppose [...] a person to have enjoyed his sight for thirty years, and to have become perfectly acquainted with colours of all kinds except one particular shade of blue, for instance, which it never has been his fortune to meet with. Let all the different shades of that colour, except that single one, be placed before him, descending gradually from the deepest to the lightest; it is plain that he will perceive a blank, where that shade is wanting, and will be sensible that there is a greater distance in that place between the contiguous colours than in any other. Now I ask, whether it be possible for him, from his own imagination, to supply this deficiency, and raise up to himself the idea of that particular shade, though it had never been conveyed to him by his senses? I believe that there are few but will be of opinion that he can [...] .[28]

There is little doubt that the person described in Hume's story will indeed be able to imagine the shade after having seen the series from

---

[27] Suppose I have some ability to 'read the mind' of my conversational partners. (I do not know how I would do it, nor that the idea is even coherent, but let this pass for the sake of argument.) In this case, my way of understanding would be quite remarkable, but there would be nothing extra remarkable about my ability to understand expressions I never heard before. I understand them, because I learn what they mean on the spot from others.

[28] Hume (1748), p. 21.

84   *Problems of Compositionality*

which it was missing.[29] Let us also grant—although anybody with the slightest doubts about extreme empiricism should remain doubtful about this—that the person could not have done so before, due to his lack of experience with regard to that particular shade. The person after having seen the series of shades is in a peculiar situation: he is able to raise up to himself the idea of the shade, which shows that in some sense he is familiar with the shade, but when he in fact imagines the idea, he has an experience he never had before. What can explain this?

The clue lies in the arrangement of the shades. Suppose the shades were placed next to each other without any easily recognizable order. Then, it seems to me, it would be impossible for a person without extraordinary abilities to imagine the one that is missing. But if the arrangement is familiar, like the one from the darkest to the lightest, one can recognize that something is missing, and also have a sense what it is that is not present. One does not know what the shade is like, before having imagined it, but one knows what it must be like.

Things are roughly similar in the case of language. There is some sort of pattern that complex expressions fit into, and this pattern plays an essential role in our understanding them. The pattern is constituted by the 'repeatable features' that Davidson mentioned in the second quote above. This much is indeed uncontroversial. However, this does not yield anything like the modest principle of understanding. The problem is that we do not know what are the repeatable features in virtue of which we grasp the meanings of complex expressions. I think the following principle is more or less self-evident:

Weak Principle of Understanding: We understand a complex expression by grasping certain familiar features of the expression and a certain familiar pattern into which these features fit.

What requires further argument is that the familiar features are the meanings of the constituents, and that the familiar pattern they fit into is their syntactic structure. As far as I can see, there is nothing in the considerations about our abilities to understand new expressions that would give us reasons to believe that these additional theses are true.[30]

---

[29] Furthermore, he would presumably be able to recognize it, and to distinguish it from similar shades shortly after having seen the series.

[30] Both examples mentioned in the previous section conform to the weak principle of understanding. In understanding **Nf7**, we have to recognize what move this is in a chess

The Argument 85

6. SUMMARY

In this chapter I questioned the standard argument for compositionality, which I called the argument from understanding. In Section 1, I identified and tried to clarify the main premise of the argument, and uncovered two of its implicit premises. One of the implicit premises is the claim that understanding an expression is grasping its meaning. In Section 2, I noted that—given the commitment to the second dogma about meanings—the premise is only available for those who accept a sufficiently Fregean conception of meaning. In Section 3, I argued against the strong principle of understanding, which if true, could be used as a main premise in the argument from understanding. In Section 4, I rejected another thesis, the modest principle of understanding, which is still strong enough to be the main premise in the argument, by criticizing the claim that it is required to explain the fact that we can understand complex expressions we have never heard before. Finally, in Section 5, I tried to show that the reason the modest principle of understanding sounds so plausible is that it is easily confused with a self-evident truth, the weak principle of understanding. The conclusion of the chapter is that the argument from understanding is not convincing.

---

game. When we do this, we grasp what N, f, and 7 mean, and a certain pattern into which they fit within a whole description of a game. In understanding 372, we have to identify the number this expression stands for. When we do this, we grasp what 3, 7, and 2 mean, and a certain pattern into which they fit which, as I argued, might be different than the pattern suggested by the syntax of the expression.

CHAPTER 4

Adjectives in Context

1. THE CONTEXT THESIS

It is uncontroversial that the meaning of a complex expression *depends* on the meanings of its constituents and on the way the constituents are combined. What *is* controversial is the claim that the meaning of a complex expression depends *only* on these features, which is what the principle of compositionality says. In many cases, what a complex expression means seems to be determined partly by facts about the *context* of its utterance. Practically all objections to the principle of compositionality are based on the phenomenon of context-dependency.

I take the context of utterance to be a wide and heterogeneous collection of facts concerning the linguistic and non-linguistic environment of a particular use of an expression. It includes facts about the time and the location of the utterance, facts about the speaker, the hearer, and the salient objects around them, facts about their shared background knowledge, and about the form and content of the conversation they had before the utterance in question was made. An expression is context-dependent if and only if it can have different meanings when uttered in different contexts.

There are many cases when we *seem* to be presented with context-dependent expressions, but in fact we are not. Consider the following examples. Suppose we are interested in what (1) and (2) mean:

(1) The farmer had enormous ears.

(2) Sinking boats can be entertaining.

87

88   *Problems of Compositionality*

It is clear that their meaning depends on the context. (1) and (2) might be embedded in the following ways:

(1a) I met a farmer at the Iowa State Fair who was very funny-looking. The farmer had enormous ears.

(1b) I met a farmer at the Iowa State Fair who was selling the nicest corn I have ever seen. The farmer had enormous ears.

(2a) I should stop digging this hole in the bottom of this ship but I cannot resist the temptation. Sinking boats can be entertaining.

(2b) I should stop watching sea battles on video but I cannot resist the temptation. Sinking boats can be entertaining.

According to the most plausible interpretation, (1a) is about certain parts of the farmer's head, while (1b) is about heads of corn; (2a) is about my activity of sinking boats, while (2b) is about boats that are sinking.

These cases cause no problem for the defender of compositionality. The illusion that we have expressions with multiple meanings arises because our ordinary *notation* is ambiguous. 'The farmer had enormous ears' can be true or false, because ' 'The farmer had enormous ears' ' (and hence '(1)', which is a name used according to the same conventions as quotation names) refers ambiguously. Similarly, ' 'Sinking boats can be entertaining' ' refers to two different sentences.[1]

---

[1] I use three different quotation marks in the dissertation. An expression *e* between single quotes is a (possibly ambiguous) name for *e*. I also use the iterated single quote to name quotation names of expressions. Double quotes differ from iterated single quotes in appearance: in the case of iterated single quote I leave a space between the single quotes, in the case of double quotes I do not. Double quotes are strictly speaking not quotation devices: the expression between the double quotes is used, not mentioned. The following examples are illustrative:

(i) 'Cambridge' refers (ambiguously) to the cities Cambridge, England and Cambridge, Massachusetts.

(ii) ' 'Cambridge' ' refers to an ambiguous quotation name which is used in (i).

(iii) According to a friend of mine, "Cambridge is a reasonably lively place." He probably has Cambridge, Massachusetts in mind.

These conventions are not supposed to be taken as a sort of analysis of how quotation is ordinarily used in English. I have grave doubts about the uniform use or coherence of ordinary quotation marks. For a recent attempt to give a unified treatment for the use of quotation marks, see Capellen and Lepore (1997). For detailed criticism of this view, cf. Elugardo (1999), Pietroski (1999) and Stainton (1999).

Adjectives in Context 89

To make my point clear, I will introduce a notational convention: I will continue to use the roman font in the ordinary way, and I will use expressions in the typewriter font with indices as disambiguated symbols. Quotation and other standard names of expressions are unambiguous in the typewriter notation. So, I claim that ' 'The farmer had enormous ears' ' refers ambiguously to the sentences 'The farmer had enormous ears$_1$' and 'The farmer had enormous ears$_2$', and that ' 'Sinking boats can be entertaining' ' refers ambiguously to the sentences 'Sinking boats can be entertaining$_1$' and 'Sinking boats can be entertaining$_2$'. What is the justification for these claims?

In the case of (1) the justification is that ' 'ear' ' refers to two distinct lexical items. According to the *Oxford English Dictionary*, ear$_1$ is "the organ of hearing in men and animals", whereas ear$_2$ is "a spike or head of corn". Etymologically the two words are completely unrelated: 'ear$_1$' comes from the Old English 'éare', and is connected to the Latin 'auris'; 'ear$_2$' comes from the Old English 'éar' and is connected to the Latin 'acus'. It is a historical coincidence that they are spelled the same way: in other languages the corresponding words have different spellings.

In the case of (2) the justification for the claim that we are dealing with two different expressions is that the linear order of 'sinking' and 'boats' disguises structural differences. This fact becomes apparent, once the modal auxiliary is removed from (2): one has to say either 'Sinking boats is entertaining' or 'Sinking boats are entertaining'.[2]

So, context plays a role in determining which expression a given sequence of phonemes stands for. The interpretation of a certain utterance requires two steps: one first has to associate expressions with segments of the sequence of phonemes, and then assign meanings to the expressions. The first step is a matter of recognition, and is strictly speaking not a semantic issue. The principle of compositionality is a constraint on what is assigned to complex expressions in the second step of the interpretation process, but it says nothing about the first. So, the cases displayed in (1 a–b) and (2 a–b) are not cases of context-

---

[2] Idioms can be treated in a similar way. The concatenation of 'kick', 'the', and 'bucket' corresponds to two different expressions. One of them is a genuine complex expression, whose meaning is determined compositionally; the other, despite its misleading syntactic complexity, is not. It is a simple expression whose meaning is idiomatic. Syntax can provide evidence for the analysis. Cf. Chomsky (1980), pp. 149–53.

90 *Problems of Compositionality*

dependency *of an expression*. They can be called instances of *metalinguistic context-dependency*.[3]

However, not all influence of the context of utterance on meaning is metalinguistic. Consider the following examples:

(3) Some basketball players are giants.

(4) Some book caused a lot of harm.

What (3) and (4) mean is fixed partly by the context in which they are uttered: in isolation, it is not determined what these sentences say. If a giant is supposed to be a "legendary being of great stature and strength and of more than mortal but less than godlike power" then (3) is false, but if it is merely "a living being of great size", it is clearly true. (4) could be true because a group of firemen became converted by the writing of a pyromaniac, or because some thick volume fell on someone's head. In the first case it is "a long literary composition" that (4) is about, while in the second it is "a set of written, printed, or blank sheets bound together".[4]

It would be groundless to say that there are really two words in English: '$giant_1$' and '$giant_2$'. Neither semantic intuition, nor etymology would support such a claim. The two meanings seem to be closely related, and they both come from the Greek 'γιγα′ς'. It seems to be a natural phenomenon of human languages that words possess meanings that are related in metaphorical ways. To say that we *must* say that the two meanings are associated with different expressions seems to me to be question begging. The case is even clearer with regard to 'book': it is clearly not a historical coincidence that English uses the same sequence of phonemes to refer to abstract books and their

---

[3] * In Stanley and Szabó (2000) we used a different terminology, which seems to me now preferable. First, we distinguished between two sorts of expressions: *phonetic* and *grammatical*. A phonetic expression contains certain sounds in a certain linear order, but how exactly the relevant segments of sound sequence correspond to the lexicon and how their order translates to grammatical structure plays no role in individuating the phonetic expression itself. By contrast, a grammatical expression is either a lexical item or constructed from such items through syntactic rules. In speaking to each other, we *articulate* phonetic expressions and thereby *utter* grammatical ones. Context plays a *grammatical role* in providing the proper lexical and syntactic analysis of the sentence articulated on a given occasion.

[4] The definitions are from the *Webster Dictionary*.

Adjectives in Context 91

concrete instances.[5] 'Giant' and 'book' are *polysemous* expressions, i.e.
' 'giant' ' and ' 'book' ' refer unambiguously, but 'giant' and 'book'
have multiple meanings that are closely associated.[6]

Even if one accepts that (3) and (4) are cases of genuine context-
dependency, they are still unproblematic from the point of view of the
principle of compositionality. The sentences have multiple meanings
because they have a constituent whose meaning depends on the
context. This is clearly not in conflict with the principle of
compositionality, since 'giant' and 'book' are presumably not complex
expressions. These examples are cases of *lexical* context-dependency:
context plays a role in determining what the constituents of a complex
expression mean in a given utterance, but it plays no additional role in
determining what the complex expression means.

It is an open question whether all alleged cases of context-
dependency that arise in possible human languages can be treated in
one of the two ways mentioned. If they are all either metalinguistic—
where context plays a role in determining what expression a given
sequence of phonemes stands for, but not in determining what that
expression means, or lexical—where context plays a role in
determining what the simple constituents of a complex expression
mean, but no additional role in fixing the meaning of the complex—
then context-dependency is not a threat to compositionality. I will call
the claim that this is indeed the case the *context thesis*:

Context Thesis: The meaning of an expression depends on context only
insofar as the meanings of its constituents do.

According to the context thesis the context-dependency of a complex
expression must be indirect. Once one has fixed what the simple
constituents mean in a given context, the way in which the meaning of
the complex expression depends on the context is also fixed. As before,

---

[5] * I no longer think that it is clear that 'book' refers ambiguously to tokens or types. I
think the option of denying that 'book' can refer to tokens has its attractions. Defenders
of such a position have to provide a pragmatic explanation how a sentence like 'I have a
book in my left hand' can communicate something true, even though it expresses a
necessary falsehood. In my Szabó (1999) I discuss the plausibility of such a view.
[6] Unfortunately, there is no terminological unity in linguistics concerning types of
ambiguity. I prefer the following definitions. A linguistic type (a phoneme or a sequence
of phonemes) is *ambiguous* if it has more than one meaning. If an ambiguous linguistic
type stands for a single expression, it is *polysemous*; otherwise it is *homonymous*.

92   *Problems of Compositionality*

the modal force of 'depends' in the context thesis should be understood as quantification over possible human languages.[7]

In the following sections, and in the next chapter, I will look at concrete challenges to the context thesis. The first case—discussed in this chapter—is that of context-dependent adjectives.

2. THE COLOR OF A PAINTED LEAF

In a recent paper, Charles Travis argues that many different things might be said with the same words, even if the subject-matter of the claims remains the same:

> As an arbitrary example, consider the words 'The leaf is green', speaking of a given leaf, and its condition at a given time, used so as to mean what they do mean in English. How many distinct things might be said in words with all that true of them? Many. That emerges when we note that one might speak either truth or falsity in such words, if the leaf is the right way. Suppose a Japanese maple

---

[7] I did not mention indexicals, which are regarded as the most common examples of context-dependent expressions. This is because it is unclear whether they provide examples where the *meaning* of an expression depends on the context. Surely, whether a sentence containing an indexical is true or not depends on the context of the utterance. However, it is not clear that one should say that the meaning of these sentences is also context-dependent. Consider the sentence 'I have never been to Alexandria.' According to the second dogma about meanings, if the sentence is meaningful then given the way the world is, its meaning determines its referent. There are three possibilities: (i) the sentence is not meaningful, (ii) the sentence is meaningful, but it is not what I called in Section 3 of Chapter 2 a genuine sentence, i.e. an expression whose referent is a truth value, (iii) the sentence is a meaningful genuine sentence. These naturally correspond to three views on the context-dependence of the sentence: (i') the sentence is in itself meaningless, it acquires meaning only in the context of an utterance, (ii') the sentence has a context-independent meaning which together with the facts about Alexandria determines a context-dependent referent, e.g. a function from contexts to truth values, (iii') the sentence has a context-dependent meaning which together with the facts about Alexandria determines its context-independent referent, i.e. its truth value. The differences among these views are partly terminological, partly substantive, and I will not try to decide here which one is correct. What is important from the point of view of the context thesis is that each is fully compatible with the context thesis. What is important is only that whatever one says about the sentence, the same should hold about the indexical expression in it. If one subscribes to (i'), one should say that the indexical in the sentence is also meaningless in itself; if one subscribes to (ii'), one should say that the meaning of the indexical is context-independent, and if one subscribes to (iii'), one should say that the meaning of the indexical is context-dependent. These conditional requirements seem to me not to be objectionable. Therefore, I believe that indexicals present no challenge to compositionality.

Adjectives in Context

leaf, turned brown, was painted green for a decoration. In sorting leaves by colour, one might truly call this one green. In describing leaves to help identify their species, it might, for all the paint, be false to call it that. So words may have all the stipulated features while saying something true, but also while saying something false. Nothing about what it is to be green decides whether the colour of a thing is the way it is with, or the way it is without the paint. What being green is is compatible with speaking either truth or falsity in calling the leaf green. For all that, the painted leaf is as it is sometimes, but not other times, said to be in calling it green.[8]

What the example shows is subject to interpretation. Let me start with what is uncontroversial. First, the truth value of an utterance of 'The leaf is green' made about the painted leaf depends on the context. Roughly, the utterance is true if it is made when one is sorting leaves for decoration, and false if it is made when one is trying to identify the species of the leaf. Second, the sequence of phonemes uttered in the two scenarios stand for the same unique sentence, i.e. ' 'The leaf is green' ' refers unambiguously to the sentence 'The leaf is green'. Consequently, that sentence must say different things in these two scenarios; the example is not an instance of metalinguistic context-dependency.

To these two obvious claims Travis adds a more problematic third one, namely, that the words 'leaf' and 'green' were used in both cases "so as to mean what they do mean in English", which is presumably something fixed. If he is right, the case of the painted leaf threatens the context thesis: the meaning of 'The leaf is green' depends on context, even though the meaning of its constituents does not.

The obvious reply is to reject the claim that 'green' really means the same in the two utterances. Since 'green' is context-dependent, it is simply misleading to stipulate that it be used in both contexts to mean what it does in English. There is no such thing as *the* meaning of 'green', just as there is no such thing as *the* meaning of 'giant' or 'book'. But there are two problems with this reply. The first is that according to Travis the example was merely illustrative, and the phenomenon has nothing to do with specificities of 'green'. The second is that 'green' does not seem to be a polysemous word. So, if it is to be

---

[8] Travis (1994), pp. 171–2.

94   *Problems of Compositionality*

a context-dependent expression, it must be of a different type than the ones considered in the previous section.

According to Travis, the example of painted leaf can be easily generalized:

> The words 'is green', while speaking of being green, may make any of indefinitely many distinct contributions to what is said in words of which they are part. The above variation is illustrative. The same holds of any English predicate. The fact that 'is green' speaks of being green does not alone decide what is required for a thing to be as it, on a speaking, says a thing to be. Similarly for whatever else words speak of.[9]

I think this is an overstatement. If one uses the sentence 'The number is even', talking about the number four, the sentence expresses a truth. One cannot construct some special scenario where due to some camouflage similar to the painting of the leaf 'The number is even' says something false.

There is a trivial way that the example can be generalized to practically all non-mathematical and non-logical predicates. Take the sentence 'The book is a novel'. There are all sorts of borderline cases, like longish short-stories, modern epics written in free verse, etc. Let the phrase 'the book' refer to (or describe uniquely) some such entity. Then there are scenarios where the sentence is true according to the contextual norm, and others where it is false. This is not especially interesting, since it does not threaten the context thesis: intuitively, whenever the meaning of 'The x is P' is vague, it is because the meaning of P can be sharpened in more than one way. What is challenging about the example of the painted leaf is that it is independent of problems of vagueness. Even if a brown maple leaf is painted the most paradigmatic green one can imagine, the problem whether the leaf is green remains.

If we neglect vagueness, however, Travis's example is not widely generalizable. There are indeed different scenarios where the sentence 'The liquid is water' is about the same substance, but has different truth values. However, all these are such that the stuff must be some borderline case, say, containing some other chemicals besides H_2O.

---

[9] Travis (1994), p. 172.

Adjectives in Context 95

Speaking of some quantity of clean water in a glass, 'The liquid is water' expresses a truth, no matter what the speaker thinks of the substance, or what the purpose of her statement is.

So, we can conclude that the kind of context-dependency that we see in 'The leaf is green' is *not* universal: 'The number is even' or 'The liquid is water' are rather similar sentences that do not have it. One can overcome the first problem concerning the suggestion that 'green' is context-dependent by pointing out that contrary to Travis's suggestion, the case of the painted leaf does not present a problem for the semantics of all predicates. Of course, it is equally obvious that the example is generalizable to many other adjectives, besides 'green'. It is quite easy to come up with parallel cases for 'The apple is red', 'The move is smart', 'The problem is interesting', or 'The soup is good'. The question is then, what is responsible for this limited phenomenon?

This brings us to the second problem concerning the suggestion that 'green' is a context-dependent adjective. 'Green' cannot be a polysemous word. What we find in the *Webster Dictionary*—alongside the non-literal meaning specifications, which are irrelevant here—is the barely exciting information: something is green if it is "of the color green". There are no numbered subentries in the entry that could give us a clue what the different possible meanings are, and we see clearly that this is not a shortcoming of the dictionary. The different meanings cannot be listed because their list is open-ended.

The question is whether a convincing story can be told about *how* the meaning of 'green' and other adjectives is supposed to depend on the context. In the rest of this chapter, I will present the outlines of an account of the semantics of a large class of context-dependent adjectives which—I will argue—includes 'green'.

3. PROBLEMS WITH 'GOOD'

It is an interesting fact that contemporary views on the semantics of adjectives evolved in a debate that started in moral philosophy. In their effort to articulate theories about what goodness consists in, philosophers turned to questions about the meaning of 'good'. 'Good' is an adjective with some peculiar characteristics, so any analysis of its meaning had to say something about the interpretation of adjectives in general as well as about the semantic features that distinguish 'good' from less problematic adjectives, like 'round' or 'tall'.

96   *Problems of Compositionality*

One of the important features of 'good', and of most other adjectives, is that they can occur both in *predicative* positions, as in 'This book is good' or in 'Today the weather is good', and in *attributive* positions, as in 'Many good books are on the table' or 'We have good weather today'. The difference can be characterized syntactically: in the former cases, the adjectives are complements of verb phrases[10], while in the latter cases, they are complements of noun phrases. The former cases seem to suggest that 'good' is a predicate, while the latter that it is a predicate-modifier. Which of these indications is to be taken seriously is a question that might affect the way in which we make sense of judgments to the effect that an act, a person, or a state of affairs is good.

There is a certain difficulty about pronouncements that 'good' is a predicate, or that it is a predicate-modifier. I regard categories like 'noun', 'verb', 'determiner', 'pronoun', 'adjective', or 'sentence' as syntactic, and categories like 'predicate', 'connective', 'quantifier', 'predicate-modifier' and 'variable', or 'formula' as logical. These logical categories, though they are syntactic categories of certain formalized languages, are certainly not syntactic categories of English.[11] But what is it supposed to mean that an expression of English belongs to a syntactic category of some *other language*?

One way to understand such claims is as being about *logical forms*. I take the logical form of an expression e in a natural language L to be an expression e' in a suitable formalized language L' which has the same *logical properties* as e. L' must have a clear, and well-understood semantics, and so e' can be used to illuminate and explain the inferential behavior of e in L.

I would like to steer between an extremely weak and an extremely strong conception of logical form. According to the weak conception, the only criterion that we might use to evaluate the adequacy of a certain logical form is whether it gets all the inferences right. This would mean that we can assign the same logical form to any two sentences of English that are logically equivalent. But surely, we should not ascribe 'Snow is falling' and 'Snow is falling and snow is falling'

---

[10] * Or, if we follow the terminology of current syntactic theory, complements of *inflectional phrases*.

[11] * What makes a category syntactic is that we can determine which expressions belong to that category through morpho-syntactic means.

Adjectives in Context 97

the same logical form. We expect more than material adequacy from logical forms. They should enable us to explain why certain natural language inferences which might seem to be valid on the basis of some superficial similarity to other inferences, are in fact invalid. They should be useful in *explaining* why certain inferences fail.

The strong conception of logical form requires that an expression and its logical form be synonymous, i.e. that the interpretation of the logical form should tell us *everything* about the meaning of the natural language expression. This demand might be based on a conception of meaning according to which the inferential properties of expressions exhaust their semantic properties, so if we can fully explain the nature of the former using a suitable logical form, we thereby explain everything about the latter. I do not know whether this claim is well-grounded.[12] I favor the view according to which logical forms provide us with a *partial* account of the semantics of natural language expressions.

So, to call 'good' a predicate (or to say that the semantic category for 'good' is that of predicate) is to say that in the logical form of English sentences containing the word 'good', we always find the same corresponding predicate. Similarly, to call it a predicate-modifier is to claim that in the logical form of English sentences containing 'good' we always find the same corresponding predicate-modifier. Using my typographical conventions, these claims can be formulated as (5) and (6):

(5) The logical form of 'good' is the predicate $\texttt{good(x)}$'

(6) The logical form of 'good' is the predicate-modifier $\texttt{(good(P))(x)}$'

(I use the typewriter font for logical forms, which is the notation introduced in the previous section to indicate the lack of ambiguity. Given that we use logical forms to *clarify* and *explain* the logical

---

[12] * See footnote 12 in Chapter 3 and the preceding discussion of entailment for one source of this concern. Another source is that the so-called semantic features are interpreted, but do not give rise to logical inferences. For example, the fact that the word 'table' is associated with the semantic feature [INANIMATE] does not mean that the inference 'There is a table in the room, therefore, there is an inanimate object in the room' is valid. Semantic features appear to give rise to *default inferences*, not to *logical inferences*.

98 *Problems of Compositionality*

behavior of natural language expressions, the demand that the languages of logical forms be free of ambiguity seems to me to be reasonable. If I had the goal of absolute precision, I would use corner quotes whenever I mention logical forms containing free variables. Since I don't, I won't.)

G. E. Moore claimed in *Principia Ethica* that 'good' is a predicate that expresses a simple property. Certainly, there is a *prima facie* plausibility in the idea that 'good' expresses goodness, like 'hard' hardness or 'green' greenness. If there is no reason to think otherwise, we can suppose that expressions in the same grammatical category have the same *kind* of semantic values.

A semantic analysis based on Moore's suggestion regards the predicative occurrences of 'good' as paradigm cases and treats sentences containing attributive occurrences as complexes built up from simpler sentences in which there are only predicative occurrences. According to Moore something is a good book if and only if it is good and it is a book.[13] One way to implement these ideas is to say that the logical form of (7) is (7′), where the language of logical forms is a formalized extensional first-order language:

(7) Susanne is a good dancer (7′) $\text{dancer}(\text{Susanne}) \land \text{good}(\text{Susanne})$

There is an argument presented by Peter Geach in his article 'Good and Evil' showing that this simple Moorean analysis cannot be the right one.[14]

(7) Susanne is a good dancer	(7′) $\text{dancer}(\text{Susanne}) \land \text{good}(\text{Susanne})$
(8) Susanne is a pianist	(8′) $\text{pianist}(\text{Susanne})$
(9) Susanne is a good pianist	(9′) $\text{pianist}(\text{Susanne}) \land \text{good}(\text{Susanne})$

The inference is certainly invalid; someone can be a good dancer and a pianist without being a good pianist. This seems to be a problem for Moore, since according to his analysis as displayed on the right, the

---

[13] One of the many passages where Moore endorses this view is the following: "For 'good conduct' is a complex notion: all conduct is not good; for some is certainly bad and some may be indifferent. And on the other hand, other things, beside conduct, may be good; and if they are so, then, 'good' denotes some property, that is common to them and conduct ..." Moore (1903), p. 2.

[14] Cf. Geach (1956).

Adjectives in Context

inference is valid. So at least one of the translations from the English sentences to the logical formalism must be incorrect.

The translation relied on four assumptions. Two of them—that in the logical form of (8) a one-place predicate is applied to an individual name, and that (7) and (9) have similar logical forms—seem to be uncontroversial. The more vulnerable assumptions are that logical forms are extensional, and that 'good' is a one-place predicate.[15] Geach's argument shows that one must give up at least one of these.

Geach's idea was to regard 'good' as a predicate-modifier rather than as a predicate. On this approach, the attributive occurrences are the paradigm cases and the predicative occurrences must be explained away. To give an account of them, one has to assume that they are elliptical attributive occurrences. Thus the sentence 'These gloves are good' is usually to be understood as 'These gloves are good gloves'. Although this is a natural interpretation of the sentence, in certain situations it is incorrect. For example, if the sentence is uttered by someone who wanted to clean the windows and was looking for some piece of cloth appropriate for that purpose, the suggested analysis would fail. In this situation the sentence is to be understood as saying 'These gloves are good pieces of cloth for cleaning the windows'. This example brings out the way in which pragmatic considerations related to the context of the utterance determine how to complete an elliptical sentence containing an attributive occurrence of 'good'. In any case, according to Geach something is good if and only if there is an appropriate noun N such that that thing is a good N.[16]

One way to build Geach's idea into a semantic analysis would be to assign $(7'')$ to (7) as its logical form, where the language of logical forms remains extensional. Here the semantic value of a predicate-modifier is a function that maps predicate extensions to predicate extensions.

---

[15] Theoretically, there is a fifth assumption made in assigning the logical forms. One might insist that the language of logical forms is extensional and that 'good' is a one-place predicate, but deny that the connective in $(7')$ and $(9')$ should be conjunction. However, it is clear that any other truth-functional connective which replaced it (e.g. '$\vee$' or '$\rightarrow$') would yield unacceptable logical forms.

[16] Geach endorses this view in the following passage: "Even when 'good' or 'bad' stands by itself as a predicate, and is thus grammatically predicative, some substantive has to be understood; there is no such thing as being just good or bad, there is only a being a good or bad so-and-so." Geach (1956), p. 65.

100   *Problems of Compositionality*

(7) Susanne is a good dancer   (7″) (good(dancer))(Susanne)

This translation is not subject to the previous criticism. From the assumption that the complex predicate ' (good(dancer))(x)' applies to the bearer of the name 'Susanne' it does not follow that the complex predicate ' (good(pianist))(x)' applies to her. So Geach's move blocks the inference from (7) and (8) to (9). In assigning (7″) as the logical form to (7), this analysis provides an implicit explanation *why* the inference is invalid. It goes like this: The inference is invalid, because ' (good(dancer))(x)' and ' (good(pianist))(x)' have different extensions, which, in turn, is true because 'dancer(x)' and 'pianist(x)' have different extensions. That is, Susanne can be a good dancer and a pianist, and still fail to be a good pianist, *because* there are people who are dancers and not pianists or *vice versa*. Now, this explanation cannot be right. For, the inference would be invalid even if we added the assumption that all and only dancers are pianists:

(7) Susanne is a good dancer	(7″) (good(dancer))(Susanne)
(8) Susanne is a pianist	(8″) pianist(Susanne)
(10) All and only dancers are pianists	(10″) $\forall x$(dancer(x)$\leftrightarrow$pianist(x))
(9) Susanne is a good pianist	(9″) good(pianist))(Susanne)

There is a way to get around this problem that has been popular in the last decades. The idea is that the logical forms should be drawn from an *intensional language*.[17] The interpretation of an intensional language distinguishes between (at least) two different semantic values of expressions: the extension and the intension. The extension of the expression is its ordinary semantic value, (a truth value for sentences, an object for names, a set of objects for one-place predicates, a function from sets to sets for predicate-modifiers, etc.) the intension of the expression is a function from possible worlds to its extension. One can have an intensional language where—although there are certain operators that are sensitive to the intensions of the expressions to which they are applied—quantification over possible worlds remains covert. Languages of modal logics are intensional languages of this type.

---

[17] Cf. Monatague (1970a), esp. p. 201, pp. 211–3, and Montague (1970b), esp. pp. 242–3.

Adjectives in Context 101

Alternatively, one can have an intensional language, where reference to possible worlds is explicit. In these languages there are variables ranging over possible worlds.[18]

I think intensional languages of the second type are more perspicuous, so I will use this technique to present the intensional solution to the problem posed by the inference from (7), (8), and (10) to (9).[19] The logical form of (7) is (7'''):

(7) Susanne is a good dancer   (7''') $(good(dancer))(Susanne)(w)$

In the logical form, 'w' is a variable that will be assigned the possible world with respect to which the sentence is evaluated. In most cases this is the actual world, so (7''') is true iff Susanne is among the individuals that are good dancers in the actual world. But (7) can be asserted in different contexts, when it is clear that the speaker is not talking about the actual world. For example the whole sentence could be embedded within a fictional narrative, and then 'w' would receive a different value.[20] (7) can also occur as a constituent in a complex sentence with modal operators, which are translated as quantifiers over the possible world variable.

Such a move blocks the inference from (7), (8) and (10) to (9). Even if the predicates '$dancer(x)$' and '$pianist(x)$' have the same extension in the world the speaker is talking about, they may have different extensions in other possible worlds. In that case their intensions are different, so the intensions of the complex predicates '$good(dancer)(x)$' and '$good(pianist)(x)$' may also be different functions, and therefore the expressions '$(good(dancer))(Susanne)$' and '$(good(pianist))(Susanne)$' may have different intensions. If they do, there is no reason why the sentences 'Susanne is a good

---

[18] Cf. Lewis (1970b), esp. pp. 193–200.

[19] * In doing this, I don't want to prejudge the complicated issue of ontological commitment. Philosophers tend to like non-explicit quantification over possible worlds because they believe that it fails to carry ontological commitment to those entities. I am doubtful whether pushing explicit quantification into the meta-language can help the ontologically scrupulous, but I don't want to press the issue here.

[20] * This sort of treatment of fictional discourse seems to me now wrong. Fictional worlds need not be consistent, so one cannot regard them as possible worlds. Besides, it is rather unclear how context could provide a non-actual world as a value for a world-variable.

102　　　　　　　　　　　　　　　　　　*Problems of Compositionality*

dancer' and 'Susanne is a good pianist' should have the same truth value in the possible world the speaker talks about.

Again, by assigning (7′′′) as logical form to (7), we implicitly commit ourselves to an explanation why the inference fails. The *reason* why someone may be a good dancer and a pianist without being a good pianist even if all dancers are pianists and *vice versa* is that there is another possible world where someone (she, or someone else) is a dancer, but not a pianist, or a pianist, but not a dancer. This does not sound very convincing. How could the possibility that someone is a dancer, but not a pianist have anything to do with the question whether Susanne has to be a good pianist, given that she is a good dancer and a pianist?

It is interesting to compare this with the following case. The inference from 'Susanne is a prospective dancer' and 'Susanne is a pianist' to 'Susanne is a prospective pianist' is also invalid. Here the intensional explanation says that the *reason* why someone may be a prospective dancer and a pianist without being a prospective pianist even if all dancers are pianists and vice versa is that there is another possible world where someone (she, or someone else) is a dancer, but not a pianist, or a pianist, but not a dancer. In this case the explanation is much more plausible. The failure of this inference can be explained by means of possibilities, because if someone is a prospective N, then she *may* become, or is *likely* to become an N. However, similar modal consequences cannot be drawn from the claim that someone is a good N.

4. WAYS OF BEING GOOD

The answer to the question why someone may be a good dancer and a bad pianist is quite obvious. Dancing and playing the piano are very different activities, so there is no reason why excellence in one should have anything to do with excellence in the other. In other words, if Susanne is a good dancer then she is good at dancing, good at a particular activity. This is perfectly compatible with her being quite bad at playing the piano, which is another activity. So, goodness—at least in this case—does not directly attach to Susanne; it attaches to her only through one or another description that is true of her. Some of these descriptions, is that she is a dancer or that she is a pianist, may specify certain roles, and she may be skillful, interesting, enthusiastic or well-

Adjectives in Context   *103*

descriptions, is that she is a dancer or that she is a pianist, may specify certain roles, and she may be skillful, interesting, enthusiastic or well-paid in one of her roles, but unskillful, boring, indifferent or badly paid in another. Being good at dancing and being good at playing the piano are different *ways of being good*.[21] This seems to be the correct analysis of 'good' and many other adjectives.

As it stands, this explanation is in accordance with the analysis that regards 'good' as a predicate-modifier. But such theories usually make a further step. It is often assumed that the relevant roles are fully specified by the noun to which the adjective 'good' is attached. But, as Geach noted, there are cases in which this move is problematic.

The difficulties are exemplified by sentences in which one speaks about a good event, or a good thing to happen. Geach says that such sentences often do not have a fixed meaning, since " 'event', like 'thing', is too empty a word to convey either a criterion of identity or a standard of goodness."[22] This means that according to Geach, the reason why 'good event' does not have clear truth-conditions is that 'event' does not have a clear meaning. But, surely, the meaning of 'pebble' or 'differential equation' are clear enough, and still, one does not know what to make of 'good pebble' or 'good differential equation'.[23] The meaning of the sentence 'This is a good pebble' depends on the context of its use. In a certain situation, it might mean that the pebble is good for playing marbles, in another that it is good for breaking a window.

So the noun N in a phrase 'a is a good N' is often not sufficient in determining the role in which a is supposed to be good. Is it at least always necessary? Geach certainly thinks so, since he believes that in order to interpret 'a is good', one always has to provide some suitable N that will yield the standards of goodness. I think this is implausible. Consider the scenario where students are performing an experiment in the laboratory. They are trying to produce some substance that can be used in a later experiment. The teacher points to a certain blue liquid and says to the students: 'This is good'. Is it really true that in order to interpret this, the students have to be able to come up with some noun N such that the blue liquid is a good N? It seems that even if they know

---

[21] The phrase 'way of being good' is borrowed from Thomson (1992).

[22] Geach (1956), pp. 68–9.

[23] I thank Judith Thomson for bringing this problem to my attention. Her discussion of it can be found in Thomson (1994). The point is also discussed in Pigden (1990).

104   *Problems of Compositionality*

know what the teacher's utterance said. The blue liquid was said to be good for the purposes of the experiment. Of course, Geach *might* reply that the noun (or, more precisely, the nominal expression) in question is something like 'stuff that can be used in a later experiment'. But why should we believe that the standards of goodness are provided by this complex noun, rather than simply by the context in which the utterance was made?

I suggest that we should return to the Moorean idea that the logical form of 'good' is a one-place predicate. Of course, there is a price for this: one certainly cannot hold a theory according to which the semantic value of 'good' is the class of good things. There may be nothing in common to all good things. However, one can say that 'good' is an *incomplete* one-place predicate, one that is associated with a set of individuals only if additional information is provided. 'Good' can be completed in many different ways; for example under one completion it is associated with a set of those individuals who are good at dancing, under another with the set of those individuals who are good at playing the piano.

The analysis I am suggesting follows Moore in the sense that it regards the predicative occurrences of 'good' as the paradigm cases. 'Good' is an incomplete expression, its semantic category is one-place predicate. I also accept Moore's analysis of the attributive occurrences: Susanne is a good dancer if and only if Susanne is good (as a dancer) and Susanne is a dancer; Susanne is a good pianist if and only if Susanne is good (as a pianist) and Susanne is a pianist. So the translation I suggest for (7) is (7''''):

(7) Susanne is $\quad$ (7'''')$\text{dancer(Susanne)} \wedge (\text{good(R)})\,(\text{Susanne})$
$\quad$ a good dancer

'R' is a variable standing for a certain role[24] in which something can be good. The value of this variable is fixed by the context in which (7) is used.

---

[24] 'Role' is used here—unlike at some other places in this dissertation—as a more or less technical term. An actor can be good in a given role. Stretching the meaning of 'role' a little, one can say that a good dancer, or pianist is good in that role. Perhaps one can say that a good pencil is good in a role, but it certainly makes no sense to say that a good nap, a good sunset, or a good painting is good in some role. The variable 'R' stands for some contextual information that specifies the incomplete predicate 'good'.

Adjectives in Context   *105*

One of the consequences of this analysis is the claim that in *some* contexts (7) could mean something different from 'Susanne is good as a dancer and she is a dancer.' And indeed, one can imagine a situation in which what is at question is her moral character, not her skill at dancing. Suppose some dancers are threatening to burn down the Met, because they are unhappy about their salary. Other dancers are trying to convince the members of the first group that burning down the Met would be a bad idea. Meanwhile the singers are having a drink in a bar, and they are discussing which of their colleagues are in which group. Most of them believe that Susanne is the leader of those who are threatening to set the building on fire. One of the singers tries to defend Susanne, and argues that unlike most of the dancers, she is actually in the second group, trying to save the building. She gives several reasons for this claim, and at the end of her argument she utters 'Susanne is a good dancer' with a strong emphasis on 'good'.

But even if there are intricate examples where the claim that Susanne is a good dancer does not mean that she is good at dancing, in normal contexts it does. This means that in order to accept (7'''') as the logical form of (7), one has to extend the notion of context introduced at the beginning of this chapter. There I said that the meaning of previous utterances may play a role in determining the meaning of an expression. Now I suggest that the meaning of certain expressions within the utterance may be part of the context that contributes to determining the meaning of other expressions within the *same* utterance. What 'good' means in (7) may depend on the meaning of 'dancer'.[25]

5. VARIETIES OF INCOMPLETENESS

The story about the semantics of 'good' told in the previous two sections has obvious implications for Travis's example concerning the color of the painted leaf. If it can be made plausible that the analysis given for 'good'—according to which its logical form is a contextually incomplete predicate—applies to many other adjectives, including 'green', then we have a semantic account of these expressions that does not violate the context thesis.

---

[25] Fortunately, there do not seem to be cases when the meaning of a noun N within a 'good N' depends on the meaning of 'good' in that phrase.

106　　　　　　　　　　　　　　　　　*Problems of Compositionality*

I do not claim that the logical form of every adjective is a contextually incomplete predicate and I will not attempt to answer the question exactly which adjectives have such logical forms. 'Susanne is a retired pianist' does not mean 'Susanne is retired (as a pianist) and Susanne is a pianist'. Some adjectives (e.g. 'utter') do not have predicative occurrences at all, so there is no reason to assume that they stand for incomplete predicates. However, I think for the vast majority of adjectives that is the correct analysis.[26]

I suggest that there are (at least) three main ways in which an adjective might be incomplete. These ways are independent, and therefore there are (at least) eight different categories.

(A) Most adjectives have comparative and superlative forms. However, this does not mean that these forms make sense for every adjective. For example, a function is either differentiable or it is not. Some of them are twice differentiable, some others only once, but this feature does not make the former kind more differentiable than the latter. Some of Aristotle's works are lost, others are not. There are disputed cases, some of the works that are held to be original might be falsifications, and there may even be some books that are widely believed to be lost, but are actually hidden in some secret library in northern Italy. Still, we do not say that some of Aristotle's works are more lost than others. There are also adjectives that can often be used in their comparative or superlative forms, but for which this usage is not always legitimate. A good example is 'entertaining'. We often compare things in the sense of how entertaining they are, but we do not presuppose that such a comparison could always be made between any two things to which the adjective is applicable.

Following standard terminology I will call the adjectives that have a universally applicable comparative form *scalar* adjectives. 'Tall', 'heavy', 'fast', 'expensive', 'old,' etc. are scalar adjectives, 'mortal', 'delicious', 'secret', 'forgotten' etc. are not. If an adjective A is scalar,

---

[26] Predicative analyses of certain adjectives are also suggested in Kamp (1975) and in Higginbotham (1985). Kamp restricts the scope of such analyses to adjectives that are extensional in the sense that whenever they have an attributive occurrence in a sentence without modal operators, the modified noun can always be replaced by a co-extensional expression *salva veritate*. So he does not regard 'good' as a predicate. Higginbotham phrases his suggestion in terms of a certain generalization of Chomsky's Θ-Criterion. His logical forms are more complex, and this enables him to extend his approach to all adjectives, including 'fake', or 'retired'. I advocate a theory that represents a solution falling between Kamp's and Higginbotham's positions.

Adjectives in Context 107

then for any two things that are *A* it must either be that they are equally *A*, or one is more *A* than the other. In other words any two individuals that are *A* have to be comparable in terms of *A-ness*.[27]

The contextual dependency of scalar adjectives is quite straightforward. In order to get a normal predicate extension, a reference class has to be specified and the adjective has to be interpreted with respect to this class. Short basketball players are usually tall people, light whales are heavy animals and—for many of us—cheap airplane tickets to Europe can be very expensive gifts. There is a uniform way to characterize the reference class, by using the preposition 'as'. So, someone can be short as a basketball player, but tall as a person, something can be light as a whale, but heavy as an animal; and something can be cheap as an airplane ticket to Europe, but expensive as a gift. Whether or not the preposition 'as' can be attached to the adjective is a good first test for whether it is a scalar adjective or not.

It is important to notice that the preposition 'as' is not always used to fix a reference class. A sentence like, 'Susanne is well-paid as a dancer' can mean that Susanne gets a good salary relative to other dancers, but also that Susanne, doing that particular job (maybe among other things) receives a high salary relative to some contextually salient reference class (maybe the class of employed people).

(B) Intuitively, some adjectives stand for properties that are always instantiated in the same way, and some for properties that can be realized in many different ways. There is just one way to be round; if something is round it must have a particular shape. However, there are many ways to be intelligent. One can be intelligent in solving crossword puzzles, in writing computer programs, in understanding poetry, in not trusting certain unreliable people and in countless other ways.

I will call adjectives that express properties that can be instantiated in various ways *cluster* adjectives. 'Large', 'careless', 'reliable', 'interesting', 'profitable,' etc. are cluster adjectives, 'four-legged',

---

[27] * This criterion is probably too strong, as the case of 'expensive' well illustrates. We do suppose that any two things that have price, are comparable in terms of this price. But problems arise when there is no single currency, in which these comparisons could be made. So, for example, we are not sure that there is a fact of the matter which was more expensive: the construction of the Taj Mahal or the construction of Versailles. Still, in *most* cases, we suppose that a comparison can be made.

108 *Problems of Compositionality*

'distant', 'round', 'hot', 'transparent,' etc. are not. One has to specify some way in which the property can be instantiated in order to interpret a cluster adjective. Something can be large in length, but small in breadth; someone can be careful in driving, but careless in playing chess; or interesting in conversation, but boring in a paper. We can use the preposition 'in' or 'at' to characterize ways of realization; a good *prima facie* test for whether an adjective is a cluster adjective is whether such prepositions can be attached to it.

Like 'as', the preposition 'in' has very different uses and some of them can be misleading when one tries to decide whether a given adjective is a cluster adjective. One can truly say 'Vodka is expensive in Sweden and in Canada', but this does not mean that there are two ways of being expensive.

(C) Most adjectives stand for properties of individuals that are in some sense independent of us. Though some philosophers might disagree, I think rocks are rigid no matter who, if anybody, observes them. On the other hand if all living beings had a radically different structure, then certain chemicals would not be fatal. To find out whether a certain pill is fatal, one has to identify the range of organisms under consideration. A pill might be fatal for dogs, but not for cats; it might be fatal for me, but completely innocuous for you. This means that the fatality of the pill is a property that can be relativized to kinds and even to individuals.

I will call adjectives expressing properties that can be relativized in various ways to kinds and/or individuals *relative* adjectives. 'Lucky', 'delicious', 'readable', 'superfluous', and 'fitting' are relative adjectives; 'homogeneous', 'sharp', 'derivable', 'dark', and 'rhythmic' are not.

When interpreting relative adjectives, it has to be specified to whom the adjective is relativized. A particular event can be fortuitous for me, but not for others; an exercise can be superfluous for the expert and crucial for the novice, the outcome of an election may be lucky for one party, but not for the country.

The preposition 'for' is a good indicator that an adjective is relative. However, 'for' has uses that have nothing to do with relativity. A good example is the sentence 'A large van is useful for moving furniture'.

These distinctions are certainly neither sharp nor unproblematic. Still, I think they are intuitive and represent three possible ways in

Adjectives in Context   *109*

which an adjective can be incomplete. It is certain that none of these distinctions can be reduced to the others, since there are adjectives in all eight subclasses defined by the three distinctions.

	Scalar	**Cluster**	**Relative**	**Examples**
I	–	–	–	round, differentiable
II	+	–	–	tall, warm
III	–	+	–	clever, reliable
IV	+	+	–	large, quick
V	–	–	+	fatal, comfortable
VI	+	–	+	expensive, time-consuming
VII	–	+	+	interesting, superfluous
VIII	+	+	+	profitable, spacious

This subcategorization shows what kind of specification is required to arrive at a context-independent predicate for the particular adjectives. For example 'clever *at* doing cross-word puzzles', 'time-consuming *as* a short-paper topic *for* me' and 'spacious *in* height *as* a living room *for* people who don't mind bumping their heads every now and then' are wholly specified one-place predicates.

For predicates that have been completed, inferences of the form '*a* is an *AN*' and '*a* is an *M*', therefore '*a* is an *AM*' are valid. For example, from 'Susanne is a clever dancer' and 'Susanne is a pianist' it *does* follow that 'Susanne is a clever pianist', *provided* that e.g. the context had already specified that 'clever' is to be understood as 'clever at solving crossword-puzzles' in both the first premise and the conclusion. Of course, if only cleverness in solving crossword-puzzles is concerned, it would be quite misleading to say that Susanne is a clever dancer or a clever pianist. One should put it rather as 'Susanne, who is a dancer (pianist) is clever'. The reason for this is that the sentence 'Susanne is a clever dancer' strongly *suggests* that the kind of cleverness that is ascribed to Susanne has something to do with the fact that she is a dancer.

To which subcategory does 'good' belong? It is certainly a cluster adjective. Clearly, there are many ways in which something can be good. A good dancer is good at dancing, a good pianist is good at playing the piano. This kind of underspecification of the adjective 'good' was already mentioned and recognized to be the cause for the failure of some inferences in the previous section.

110   *Problems of Compositionality*

It is also reasonably clear that 'good' is not a scalar adjective. Even if we specify a way of being good, say 'good as a pianist', we are quite reluctant to apply the comparative form of 'good' universally. It does not seem to be the case that for any two people, either they are equally good as pianists or one is better than the other. People may well be incomparable in terms of how good they are as pianists.

The question whether 'good' is relative is much more complicated. There is *prima facie* inclination to think that it is, since something can be good for certain individuals, but bad for others. But there is a difficulty here. It is intuitively acceptable to say that all goodness is goodness in a way, but it is not as clear that all goodness is goodness for some individual, or group of individuals. Can something be good without being good for anyone (or anything)? I certainly think that if something is comfortable, time-consuming, superfluous or difficult, then there has to be some individual (or individuals) for whom it is comfortable, time-consuming, superfluous or difficult. This is much less obvious in the case of 'good'.

Consider the questions 'In what way is this good?' and 'For whom is this good?' First, there are cases when a certain type of answer is appropriate for one, but not the other question. For example if I say that the lottery numbers last week were good I make a cryptic remark. Someone may ask me both 'In what way were they good?' and 'For whom were they good?' In answering the first question I cannot merely say that the lottery numbers last week were good in *some* way; such a response is merely a refusal to answer. In order to respond, I have to identify a way of being good. (I might say, for example, that the lottery numbers were my absolutely favorite primes, and that is why they were good.) On the other hand, to give an answer to the second question, no identification is needed. It is enough to give a trivial description: the numbers were good for those who marked some of them on a lottery ticket and sent the ticket to the proper address in due time. If one claims something to be good, one ought to be able to say something nontrivial about the way in which the thing is good, but not necessarily about the individual (or individuals) for whom the thing is good.

Second, there are cases when the question 'For whom is it good?' does not make sense. If after a theater performance someone praises one of the actors by saying that he was very good, the question 'For whom was he good?' can only be interpreted as an ironical remark.

Adjectives in Context

Similarly, the fact that Susanne is good at mental arithmetic does not make the question 'For whom is she good?' interpretable.

Finally, there seem to be cases when the question 'For whom is it good?' does make sense, and it also has an appropriate answer, but the answer is that it is not good for anybody. Suppose that I promised someone before her death that I will do something. Suppose further that as far as I am able to see, this particular act is neither good nor bad for any individual I can think of. I am tempted to say that in this case it is still good to fulfill my promise. The way in which it is good can be specified: it is good in being honest. However, there does not seem to be any individual for whom the action is good. The example was created in such a way as to exclude the person to whom the promise was made and third parties from the range. One could probably argue that the action is good for me, or somehow for all of us, but I do not see why this necessarily has to be the case.[28]

Whether or not 'good' is a relative adjective has not been decisively established here, but I think the examples strongly suggest that it is not. Because the category of relative adjectives is far from being homogeneous, to clarify the issue further one should probably introduce an even more fine-grained categorization than I have presented above. Still, I conclude provisionally that 'good' is an adjective that belongs to subcategory III. It is an adjective that can be specified by specifying a way of being good. Its specification resembles more closely the specification of 'clever' or 'reliable' than the specification of 'interesting' or 'profitable'.

6. WAYS OF BEING GREEN?

How does 'green' fit into this categorization? It is certainly not a relative adjective: no matter how much one believes in the possibility of an inverted spectrum, it is incorrect to say that a leaf is green *for* me. We use color terms as if color were an objective, observer-independent feature of the world. We have another construction, namely 'seems

---

[28] The question 'For whom is it good?' should be distinguished from the question 'According to what standards is it good?' None of the objections to the universal appropriateness of the former arises with respect to the latter. Ziff (1960) argues that the adjective 'good' is used almost invariably in impersonal remarks. It is the speaker's intention when using the adjective 'good' to say something that is based on standards, not on mere opinion or guess.

112 — Problems of Compositionality

green' which is correctly used in cases when the speaker wants to express uncertainty with respect to veridicality of her subjective experience.

It is also quite clear that 'green' is not a scalar adjective. It can be *vague* whether a leaf is green or brown, but this does not make it a less green thing. One might say, that one leaf is more greenish than the other. One might also *implicate* that one leaf is more greenish than another by saying that one leaf is more green than the other. However, as we know from Grice, saying and implicating are not the same. 'Green' and 'greenish' are different adjectives, although the first can be metaphorically interpreted as the second.

Whether 'green' is a cluster adjective is more difficult to decide. It seems that we cannot speak of ways of being green in the sense in which we can talk about ways of being intelligent or good. To be green is one of the most obvious examples of a feature that is *simple*. It is often difficult to decide whether something is green because of the condition of the object, the environment, or the nature of our perceptual mechanism; there are also borderline cases, when there might be no fact of the matter whether something is green. But what it is to be green seems to exclude different kinds of instantiations.

I think this intuition is misleading. There are at least two ways in which an apple can be green: from the outside, or from the inside. In the former case, it can be ripe, in the latter it cannot. There are at least three ways in which a book can be green: due to having a green dust jacket, a green cover, or green pages. And a corridor can be green in many ways: having green walls, or green ceiling, or green carpet, or green doors, etc. An object is green if some contextually specifiable (and presumably sufficiently large) *part* of it is green. The logical form of 'green' is 'green at $P(x)$', where 'P' is a variable standing for a certain part of the object that counts in the given context of the utterance.

It seems to me that the case of the painted maple leaf fits this pattern. If one is sorting leaves for decoration, what matters is the color of the outside, if one is trying to identify the species, what matters is what we find under the camouflage. This suggests that the context-dependency that appears in Travis's example is a relatively easily characterizable kind, which fits well into the general scheme.

Adjectives in Context

7. SUMMARY

In this chapter, I argued that certain considerations about the behavior of adjectives in natural languages do not defeat the principle of compositionality. In Section 1, I identified two ways in which the meaning of a certain sequence of phonemes may depend on the context, which I called metalinguistic and lexical context-dependency. I argued that those cases that can be subsumed under one of these headings are unproblematic with respect to the principle of compositionality. Then I formulated the context thesis, according to which the context-dependency of a complex expression is always the result of the context-dependency of some of its constituents. If the context thesis is true, context-dependency does not refute compositionality. In Section 2, using an example due to Charles Travis, I constructed a challenge to the context thesis based on the behavior of 'green', and other context-dependent adjectives. In Sections 3 and 4, I argued for a semantic account which can reply to the challenge. According to the semantic analysis I outlined, most adjectives are contextually incomplete one-place predicates. In Section 5, I presented a subcategorization of these adjectives, which can help to explain the ways in which the meaning of these adjectives depends on the context in which they are used. Finally, in Section 6, I argued that 'green', and other color adjectives, fit well into this categorization. The conclusion of the chapter is that the challenge raised in Section 2 can be successfully answered.

CHAPTER 5

Descriptions in Context

1. A PARALLEL

The story told in the last chapter about the semantics of 'good' had the following structure. First, a simple Moorean account[1] was presented, according to which adjectives are—or, more precisely, have the logical form of—predicates expressing properties. Something is good if and only if the predicate 'good(x)' applies to it. Second, an anomaly was found in the Moorean account: one can be a good dancer and a pianist without being a good pianist. The reaction to this difficulty was to suggest, following Geach, that adjectives are not predicates, but predicate-modifiers. Consequently, whenever 'good' occurs in a predicative position, an appropriate noun has to be supplied in order to interpret the sentence. This means that the grammatical form of sentences such as 'Lunch today was good' is misleading: the grammatical form disguises the presence of a noun N provided by the context, which is modified by 'good'. Third, it was noted that if we have to accommodate context-sensitive parameters in the logical forms of sentences containing 'good', we might as well return to a refined version of the simple Moorean analysis: adjectives are predicates, but they usually express properties only if these parameters are somehow specified.

---

[1] When I speak of a Moor*ean*, Geach*ean*, Meinong*ean*, Russell*ian*, etc. account, I mean to suggest that the semantic theories I describe are *motivated* by the observations and arguments of these philosophers; however, not only the technicalities, but even some of the crucial notions of the presentation might be quite alien to their thought.

115

116   *Problems of Compositionality*

In this chapter I want to tell another story that has the same structure. This story concerns the semantics of descriptions. The tale begins with a simple Meinongean account, according to which descriptions are singular terms picking out an object. 'The present queen of England' refers to Elizabeth II, just as 'Elizabeth II' does. In the dramatic second act, an anomaly is found within the Meinongean account: maybe 'the present queen of England' refers, but what about 'the present king of France'? The reaction to this difficulty is to suggest, following Russell, that descriptions do not refer at all, that they are quantificational phrases. Consequently, the logical form of sentences containing descriptions differs radically from their grammatical form. Furthermore, since the sentence 'The table is covered with books' might be true even though there are many tables in the world, the context has to provide some way of restricting the domain of quantification so that it contains only one table. This leads directly to the third act, in which I will argue, that if we have to build context-sensitive parameters into the logical form of descriptions, we might as well return to a refined version of the simple Meinongean analysis.

The idea of returning to the original naive analysis has to be taken with a grain of salt in both cases. According to the theory outlined in the previous chapter, 'good' does *not* express a property: there may be nothing common in all good things. Similarly, according to the theory that I will present in this chapter, 'the present king of France' does *not* refer: there is no such thing as the present king of France.

Russell's proposal about descriptions can be understood in at least two ways. On the weaker reading, it is a thesis about the regimentation of natural language. On this interpretation, descriptions can, in certain circumstances, be *replaced* by appropriate quantificational devices. This view has been advanced by Quine among others,[2] and will not concern me in this chapter. On the stronger reading, Russell's claim directly concerns the meanings of natural language sentences. On this interpretation, recently endorsed by Neale,[3] descriptions can be

---

[2] Quine (1953) regards Russell's theory primarily "as a means of getting on in science without use of any real equivalent of the vernacular 'the'." (p. 151) Cf. also Quine (1960), pp. 183–4.

[3] According to Neale (1990), the theory "can be seen as a contribution to a purely semantical project, that of constructing an empirically adequate theory of meaning for natural language" (p. 6).

Descriptions in Context *117*

identified with a certain type of quantificational device. According to this conception, the quantificational form yields at least a perspicuous presentation of the exact truth conditions of sentences containing descriptions.[4]

My main goal in this chapter is to argue against this stronger claim. Since the claim is undoubtedly motivated by the theory of 'On Denoting', occasionally I call the theory that is developed on its basis the Russell*ian* theory of descriptions.[5]

I argue that there are good reasons to believe that a non-Russellian theory of descriptions gives a better account of the semantics of descriptions in English (and presumably in other natural languages as well) than the Russellian theory. I will try to show that the phenomena that give rise to the objections against the Russellian theory that are— according to me—decisive are related to the context thesis. Some of the participants in the debate about descriptions thought that the kind of semantic analysis I suggest is in conflict with the context thesis. Although it will be clear that this is not the case, there is a sense in which the analysis leads to a further expansion of the notion of context.

2. REFERRING AND QUANTIFYING PHRASES

Grammar tells us that descriptions are phrases whose head is a *determiner*.[6] The lexical category of determiners is quite heterogeneous; besides the indefinite and definite articles ('a(n)', 'the'),

---

[4] Neale presents an account of the logical form of sentences containing descriptions. What logical forms are, is of course, open to philosophical argument. I take them to be expressions in a formalized language which have the same logical properties as the original expression, and which can be used to explain our intuitions (including our lapses!) about logical consequence. (Cf. Section 3 of Chapter 4.) This is a stronger requirement than what most Russellian theorists would accept. My argument will not rely on this; all I assume is that the logical forms of sentences determine their truth conditions.

[5] Russell himself did not consider his theory to be about the semantics of the English articles 'a(n)' and 'the'. In particular, with respect to the uniqueness implications of definite descriptions in English he frequently expressed reservations. This is a characteristic remark from Russell (1905): "Now *the*, when it is strictly used, involves uniqueness; we do, it is true, speak of '*the* son of So-and-so' even when So-and-so has several sons, but it would be more correct to say '*a* son of So-and-so'. Thus for our purposes we take *the* as involving uniqueness" (p. 44.) Russell held the view that although the actual usage of the definite article does not correspond exactly to his theory, his semantics of definite descriptions is a fruitful *idealization* based on the language use of the speakers of English.

[6] * For this reason descriptions are categorized by some linguists as *determiner phrases*. According to other approaches to syntax descriptions are noun phrases.

118   *Problems of Compositionality*

it traditionally comprises demonstratives ('this', 'that'), quantifiers ('every', 'some', 'few', etc.), and possessive pronouns ('my', 'her', etc.), as well as certain further expressions.

A theory of descriptions in a *broad sense* would be a comprehensive semantic account of all descriptions. Such a theory does not exist, because there are at least three very poorly understood phenomena that it would have to address. These are the problems of plurals ('The cats are sleeping on the mat'), mass nouns ('The water is spinning in the bucket'), and generic sentences ('The African elephant lives in groups'). A theory of descriptions in a *narrow sense* neglects these (and maybe some other) difficulties and concentrates on simple cases. In the rest of this chapter, I will use the terms 'theory of descriptions' and 'description' only in the narrow sense.

The main question a theory of descriptions has to answer is whether the semantic behavior of indefinite and definite articles resembles the semantic behavior of some other type of determiners.[7] The two candidates that have been proposed for such an assimilation are the demonstratives and the quantifiers. I categorize theories of description into four types depending on their position on this issue. Some theories assimilate descriptions only to demonstratives, others assimilate them only to quantifiers. Then there are some theories that claim that descriptions behave sometimes like demonstratives, sometimes like quantifiers, but never in some third way. Finally some theories claim that—at least in some cases—articles behave unlike either demonstratives or quantifiers. In the rest of this section I will present these positions in more detail.

Referential Theories

Demonstratives are devices of reference. The truth or falsity of a sentence of the form 'This F is G' depends only on the properties of a certain individual, which is called the referent of 'this F'. Assimilating the articles to demonstratives amounts to the claim that descriptions are also referring phrases, hence the truth or falsity of sentences of the form 'An F is G' and 'The F is G' is also determined by the properties of a

---

[7] This is a problem of semantic categorization. It is analogous to the question considered in Chapter 4: the problem whether on the level of logical form adjectives are predicates or predicate-modifiers is the problem whether adjectives semantically resemble nouns or adverbs.

Descriptions in Context 119

particular individual.[8] To make this proposal more precise one can introduce the notion of a referring phrase:

Referring Phrase: '*Det F*' is a referring phrase if and only if the truth or falsity of a sentence of the form '*Det F is G*' is determined by the properties of a particular individual.

I will call a theory that is committed to the thesis that all occurrences of descriptions are referring phrases a *referential* theory. Probably nobody ever held such a view, though some might have thought it correct with regard to *definite* descriptions. (This is how Russell interpreted Meinong.)

Quantificational Theories

Quantifiers are devices of quantification. The truth or falsity of a sentence of the form '$Q F is G$', where 'Q' is a quantifier, depends only on how many things there are within the universe of discourse that are both F and G, neither F nor G, F but not G, and G but not F.[9] In fact, it has been extensively argued that for natural language quantifiers the truth conditions of '$Q F are G$' are fixed by the cardinalities of two sets: **F–G** and **F ∩ G**. (I am using '**F**' and '**G**' as symbols for the set of Fs and the set of Gs within the universe of discourse.)[10] Assimilating the articles to quantifiers amounts to the claim that the truth or falsity of

---

[8] The view that articles are semantically like demonstratives has some *prima facie* plausibility for the definite article. The Indo-European root of 'the' is 'so-' which is a demonstrative determiner in the nominative. The etymological links among 'this', 'that', 'there', 'then' and 'the' are still clearly sensed by most English speakers. The connection exists in languages outside the Indo-European family as well. For a study of the definite article in more than two hundred languages see Krámský (1972).

[9] * This characterization of determiners expressing binary quantification is fairly standard; cf. Keenan E. and D. Westerståhl (1997). It is equivalent to the following permutation-invariance condition. Let **F** be the set of Fs and **G** the set of Gs within the universe of discourse and let **Det** be the binary relation between subsets of the universe such that '*Det F is G*' is true iff **Det(F)(G)**. Furthermore, let π be a permutation of the universe, let $\pi\mathbf{F}=\{\pi(x):x\in\mathbf{F}\}$ and $\pi\mathbf{G}=\{\pi(x):x\in\mathbf{G}\}$. Then '*Det F is G*' is true iff **Det(πF)(πG)**.

[10] * This depends on the claim that natural language quantifiers satisfy three conditions: Isomorphism, Conservativity and Extension. It is provable that if a binary quantifier Q satisfies these three conditions then the truth conditions of '$Q F is G$' are determined by |**F–G**| and |**F ∩ G**|. For definitions of Isomorphism, Conservativity and Extension and for the proof of the relevant theorem see Keenan and Westerståhl (1997), pp. 847-58.

120 *Problems of Compositionality*

sentences of the form 'An F is G' and 'The F is G' is determined in this way.[11] Quantifying phrases can be semantically characterized as follows:

Quantifying Phrase: '*Det F*' is a quantifying phrase if and only if the truth or falsity of a sentence of the form '*Det F is G*' is determined by quantitative relations between the Fs that are Gs and the Fs that are not Gs.

Theories of description according to which all occurrences of descriptions are quantifying phrases are *quantificational theories*.

The Russellian theory of description is a quantificational theory. According to the Russellian theory, the sentences 'An F is G' and 'The F is G' are equivalent to their *Russellian expansions*:

(E_i) `∃x(F(x)∧G(x))`
(E_d) `∃x.F(x)∧∀y∀z((F(y)∧F(z))→y=z)∧∀u(F(u)→G(u))`

(I use typewriter font because (E_i) and (E_d) are often suggested to be the schematic logical forms of the schematic sentences 'An F is G' and 'The F is G', respectively.) The first conjunct in (E_d) ensures that the extension of the predicate 'F' contains at least one element, the second that it contains at most one element. These conjuncts are called the *existence* and *uniqueness* clauses of definite descriptions. The truth conditions of 'An F is G' and 'The F is G' can be presented in a way that brings out that according to the Russellian theory, the descriptions within such sentences are quantifying phrases:[12]

(T_i) The sentence 'An F is G' is true iff $|F \cap G| \geq 1$
(T_d) The sentence 'The F is G' is true iff $|F-G| = 0$ and $|F \cap G| = 1$

---

[11] In the case of indefinite descriptions, etymology favors the quantificational view. The Indo-European root of 'an' is 'oi-no-', which means one. In the non Indo-European Afghan, Chinese, Fordate, Hungarian, Jagnobi, Persian, Votapuri, Yazghulami, and dozens of other languages the same word is used for the number one and the indefinite article. Cf. Krámský (1972).

[12] * It should be emphasized that the Russellian theory is not the *only* quantificational theory of descriptions. One might assign different but still quantificational truth conditions to sentences containing indefinite and/or definite descriptions.

Descriptions in Context   *121*

Either-Or Theories

One might argue that quantificational theories are right about some occurrences of descriptions, and referential theories are right about the others. Prominent among either-or theorists are those who attach semantic significance to Donnellan's referential/attributive distinction and argue that some occurrences of definite descriptions refer.[13] Somewhat less popular, but still significant in number are those who follow Fodor and Sag in attaching semantic significance to the specific/non-specific distinction and say that certain occurrences of indefinite descriptions refer.[14] These theories abandon the claim that descriptions constitute a semantically uniform category, so I will call them *either-or* theories of description. They are committed to the thesis that some occurrences of descriptions are referring phrases, and that all other occurrences are quantifying phrases. Which are which is determined on the basis of the context in which the sentence is used.

Neither-Nor Theories

Finally, one might argue that certain descriptions can be assimilated neither to demonstratives nor to quantifiers. To understand what such a position might be like, we can consider the status of the possessives; expressions like 'my' are determiners that are neither devices of reference, nor devices of quantification. The latter is immediately clear: though I have a black coat, no numeric relation between Boolean combinations of the set of coats and the set of black things determines the truth of the sentence 'My coat is black'. 'My' is also not a device of reference, since there is no particular object whose properties determine the truth value of the sentence. If my black coat were to belong to someone else, and I had another coat instead, then the sentence would be true or false according to the color of that other coat. So there are some phrases built up from a determiner and a nominal expression that are neither referring phrases, nor quantifying phrases.[15] According to

---

[13] * For the distinction cf. Donellan (1966). For recent defense, cf. Wettstein (1981), Wettstein (1983), Recanati (1993), and Reimer (1998a).

[14] * Cf. Fodor and Sag (1982). Cf. also Chastain (1975) and Barwise and Perry (1983).

[15] The fact that 'my coat' is not a quantifier phrase in the sense defined here does not mean that it cannot be quantificational in a broader sense. If 'my coat' is just the surface form of 'the coat that belongs to me' and if the Russellian theory is correct about 'the', then the sentence 'My coat is black' has a quantificational structure after all.

122   *Problems of Compositionality*

neither-nor theories of description, at least some descriptions belong among these phrases.

These four types of theories are mutually exclusive and exhaust all possibilities. If there is such a thing as the correct semantic theory of descriptions, it must belong to exactly one of these types. All four represent coherent positions, but they are not equally plausible. For example, Russell's arguments against the referential view are compelling. Anyone accepting a referential theory will have to believe either that the present king of France, the golden mountain and the largest prime number exist—at least in *some* sense—or that certain sentences that seem to be clearly true have undetermined truth value.[16] Take for example the sentence 'The largest prime is 7'. According to the referential theories, the truth or falsity of this sentence depends *only* on the properties of the largest prime. If one believes (as most of us do) that there is no such thing as the largest prime, one is also committed to the claim that it has no properties, hence that there is nothing that would determine the truth value. But then—despite its apparent falsity—the truth value of this sentence is undetermined.

So I accept Russell's refutation of the referential view, but I do not share the commitment of many of his followers to the quantificational position. In the following sections I will develop an argument against the Russellian theory and I will try to support a version of the *neither-nor* theory.[17]

3. TWO OBJECTIONS TO THE QUANTIFICATIONAL VIEW

Objections to the quantificational theory are usually directed at its analysis of definite descriptions. The charge is that the truth conditions

---

[16] This follows from the claim that the truth or falsity of a sentence of the form 'The F is G' is *determined* by the properties of a particular individual. This implies that *there is* an individual such that its properties determine the truth or falsity of the sentence. (As in Section 5 of Chapter 1, I read 'determine' as a term indicating strong supervenience. Notice that even weak supervenience would entail that the individual exists.) One can conditionalize the thesis of referential theories, following the technique used in Section 3 of Chapter 2, when I formulated the second dogma about meaning. The weaker thesis would go as follows: Provided that the referent of a description exists, the properties of the referent determine the truth value of any sentence containing the description. This weaker version avoids the dilemma mentioned in the text, but it can be criticized on another ground. It is committed to the claim that definite descriptions are at least weakly *rigid*. However, as Kripke (1980) has argued persuasively, this is not the case.

[17] * My views have changed since. In my 'Descriptions and Uniqueness' (forthcoming b), I argue for a non-Russellian version of the quantificational view.

Descriptions in Context 123

specified by (T_d) are incorrect in some cases. Since there is no plausible alternative to (T_d) on the quantificational picture, its failure gives strong reason to doubt that any quantificational theory can be correct.[18]

Critics of Russell often emphasize the point that truth conditions are not directly attached to sentences. According to them the primary bearers of truth are *utterances* of sentences. So their target is not (T_d) itself, but its modified version $(T_d{}^*)$:

$(T_d{}^*)$ An utterance of 'The F is G' is true iff $|\mathbf{F-G}| = 0$ and $|\mathbf{F} \cap \mathbf{G}| = 1$

It is important that neither (T_d) nor $(T_d{}^*)$ excludes context from the determining factors of truth conditions. According to the quantificational theory the truth value of 'The present king of France is bald' (or the truth value of an utterance of the sentence now) depends on how many things are in the set of the *present* kings of France that are bald and in the set of the *present* kings of France that are not bald. But the cardinality of these sets depends on the date of the utterance. (More precisely: 'the set of the present kings of France that are bald' and 'the set of the present kings of France that are not bald' denote different sets at different times, and the truth or falsity of (an utterance of) the sentence depends on the cardinality of *those* sets.) In order to refute the quantificational theory, one has to argue that the context-dependency of a sentence of the form 'The F is G' transcends the context-dependency of its two non-analyzed constituents F and G. In this section I will present two objections that attempt to do exactly this.

Note that if it is true that the truth conditions of 'The F is G' depend on the context in a way that cannot be explained by an appeal to the context-dependency of F and G, we have come very close to a counterexample to the context thesis. If either of the objections work, the only refuge for a defender of the context thesis is that the meaning of the article 'the' itself depends on context.

The first objection was presented by Donnellan in his 'Reference and Definite Descriptions', where he raised three lines of criticism

---

[18] * I no longer believe this. In 'Descriptions and Uniqueness', I argue that there is no semantic distinction between indefinite and definite articles. I accept the Russellian account of indefinite descriptions, but I claim that the right hand side of (T_i) gives the correct truth conditions for 'The F is G' as well. I propose to account for implications of uniqueness associated with many (though not all) occurrences of such sentences pragmatically.

124   *Problems of Compositionality*

against $(T_d{}^*)$. First, according to Donnellan, in certain cases when we utter the sentence 'The present king of France is bald' we say something true, despite the fact that the existence clause of the definite description is violated. Such a situation might occur if the speaker misidentifies a bald person as being the present king of France, but it is clear for the audience that she is talking about that particular bald person. Second, in certain cases by uttering the sentence 'The king is bald' we express a truth, despite the fact the uniqueness clause is violated. This happens when the speaker identifies a bald person as being the only (or at least the only relevant) king, and it is clear for the audience that she is talking about that particular bald person. Third, an utterance of 'The present queen of England lives in England' may be false, despite the fact the corresponding Russellian proposition is true, if the speaker misidentified someone living in France as the queen of England, but it is clear for her audience that the speaker means that person when making the assertion.

According to Donnellan, we have to make a distinction between two different uses of definite descriptions. If a speaker uses a definite description *attributively* in an assertion, she states something about whatever fits the description. If a speaker uses a definite description *referentially* in an assertion, she uses it to enable her audience to pick out the individual she is talking about and she states something about that individual. The problematic cases for the quantificational theory are the referential cases, for in those cases the description is not supposed to tell the audience anything about an individual; its task is rather to identify one. And if the audience succeeds in picking out the right individual, then they will understand the sentence as saying something about that individual, no matter whether it actually fits the description. Donnellan's theory is an *either-or* theory: referential uses of definite descriptions are to be interpreted as referring phrases, while attributive uses of definite descriptions are quantifying phrases.[19]

---

[19] Some elements of Donnellan's criticism can be found already in Strawson (1950), and Strawson (1964). Strawson argues that when we use a sentence of the form 'The F is G', we usually have two tasks. The first is to identify a certain F that one is talking about, and the other is to say something about that individual. He calls the first task the *referring*, the second the *attributive* task. If, for some reason, the former task cannot be achieved, then the speaker failed to say anything true or false. Since no proposition was expressed, the question of truth and falsity does not arise. Strawson argues that the existence and the uniqueness conditions (together with some further conditions) are presupposed by any utterance of a sentence containing a definite description; if they are false, the referring

Descriptions in Context   *125*

The second objection can be found in Heim's 'File-Change Semantics and The Familiarity Theory of Definiteness'. Heim challenges the view that the existence and uniqueness clauses have the same status. She argues that the quantificational theory is correct with regard to the existence clause, but not with regard to uniqueness. Failure of the former leads to falsity; failure of the latter does not. One might illustrate this with an example: if someone says now in France 'The king is brave', the person says something false. However, if someone shortly before the invasion of Xerxes uttered the sentence 'The king is brave' in Sparta, what the person said is true, despite the fact that Sparta had two kings at that time.

Heim presents a semantic theory of description according to which definite descriptions have no semantic uniqueness implications.[20] She regards the task of interpreting a sequence of sentences to be quite similar to the task of the file clerk. Metaphorically speaking, the hearer must construct and continuously update certain *file-cards* to store the information conveyed by the speaker. The file-cards correspond to

---

task of the sentence cannot be achieved. (The term 'presupposition' was introduced only in Strawson (1952), pp. 184–9.) Already in Strawson (1950) he mentions that sometimes definite descriptions do not have an identifying task, and in his subsequent papers on presupposition Strawson makes the distinction between identifying and non-identifying use of definite descriptions clear. He obviously needs this distinction to account for the fact that our intuitions concerning the truth conditions of utterances of 'The present king of France does not exist' clearly favor the Russellian analysis. Similarly, the question 'Was de Gaulle the king of France?' is a completely appropriate query from a person who is in doubt as to whether de Gaulle was the king or the president of France. No presupposition is present here that someone was the king of France in de Gaulle's time. (These examples are—with slight modification—from Donnellan (1966).) So Strawson's account is a version of the *either-or* view: in some, but not all of the cases (whenever the definite descriptions have an identifying task in an assertion) the existence and uniqueness clauses associated with them are presupposed, not entailed by the sentences featuring in the assertions. Cf. Strawson (1964), p. 78.

[20] The theory presented in Heim (1983) is a slightly modified version of the one in the Chapter III of Heim (1982). A similar theory was suggested in Kamp (1981) for the treatment of indefinite descriptions and anaphoric pronouns. In its original version, Kamp's Discourse Representation Theory did not deal with definite descriptions. For later developments and extensions of this type of theory to the interpretation of sentences containing plurals and tense markers, verb phrase and sentential anaphora see Kamp and Reyle (1993) and Asher (1993). These versions of the Discourse Representation Theory accept Heim's analysis for some, but not all occurrences of definite descriptions. Cf. Kamp and Reyle (1993) pp. 248–56, Asher (1993), pp. 82–4. Another approach that is very similar in spirit is Wilson (1991). There are also versions of DRT that explicitly try to accommodate semantic uniqueness implications for all occurrences of definite descriptions. (Cf. Kadmon (1987), pp. 193–242).

126   *Problems of Compositionality*

descriptions in a text; the various conditions that hold of the individuals described by descriptions get written on these cards. The difference between indefinite and definite descriptions is merely that the former are assigned new file-cards, whereas the latter are assigned to old ones already present in the file. Indefinite and definite descriptions are characterized by the following two principles:

Novelty Principle: For every indefinite description, start a new card.

Familiarity Principle: For every definite description, update an appropriate old card.

For example, if we hear the sentence 'A man greeted a woman' we have to create two file-cards. The first one has the index '1' and will contain the following conditions: `is a man`, `greeted 2`. The second one has the index '2' and will contain the following conditions: `is a woman`, `was greeted by 1`. If the next sentence is 'The woman dropped her umbrella', an old card has to be updated and a new one has to be created.[21] The file-card with the index '2' will now contain two new conditions: `owns 3`, and `dropped 3`; the new file card has the index '3', and will contain the conditions `is an umbrella`, `is owned by 2`, and `was dropped by 2`.

Files can be regarded as logical forms.[22] Sentences of a natural language are interpreted according to this theory in two steps. First,

---

[21] The interpretation of 'her umbrella' causes a difficulty. Semanticists often make the syntactic assumption that 'her umbrella' is just the surface form of the underlying 'the umbrella of her'. This means that 'her umbrella' is a disguised definite description, so according to the Familiarity Principle it should be associated with an old file-card. It is often the case that definite descriptions are used in the beginning of a discourse. In such cases they clearly must introduce a new file-card, despite their definiteness. For example the sentence 'The president of Tadjikistan had a bad day' can be uttered in most contexts, even if it is not common ground that Tadjikistan has a president. This phenomenon is called *accommodation*. (The term was introduced in Lewis (1979).) A pragmatic theory is called for to spell out the appropriate conditions under which accommodation is a legitimate interpretative procedure. In Section 5, I will suggest a slightly different solution to the problem.

[22] Heim's notion of file-card is an explication of another notion introduced by Karttunen. Karttunen (1976) argues that indefinite descriptions introduce new *discourse referents*, and that pronouns and other definites "refer" to these discourse referents. The theory suggested by Millikan (1984) also has many features in common with Heim's view. She distinguishes between two functions of descriptions—introducing new referents and familiar referents—and argues that using the definite article with nominal expressions

Descriptions in Context   127

they have to be associated with a set of file-cards with the appropriate conditions on them. (This process was illustrated in the example above.) The next step is to assign semantic values to the logical forms. Following Tarski, Heim first defines when a certain sequence of individuals satisfies a file and then, using the notion of satisfaction, she defines truth for files. Hereby, the truth conditions of sentences are determined by translating the sentences to files and then interpreting the files. The interesting element of the definition is that the last step contains an implicit existential quantification: a file is true if and only if it is satisfied by *some* sequence of individuals. According to this interpretation process definite descriptions (like 'the woman' in the above example) do not carry any uniqueness implication. The semantic behavior of definite descriptions is somewhat similar to that of anaphoric pronouns: in order to interpret a definite description, one has to find a certain other expression in the context such that the definite description and that other expression corefer.[23,24]

Heim's theory is a *neither-nor* theory: descriptions are neither referring phrases, nor quantifying phrases. For example, the definite description 'the woman' in the above example does not belong to either of these categories. It cannot be a referring phrase, since the file-card associated with it is satisfied by *any* individual that is a woman who was greeted by a man, and dropped an umbrella that she owns. According to the definition given above, it cannot be a quantifying phrase either, since the truth or falsity of the sentence is not determined by the cardinalities of the set of women who dropped an umbrella they possess, and the set of women who did not do that. On Heim's theory, such occurrences of descriptions belong to a third semantic category. I will call expressions belonging to this type *coreferring* phrases; their

---

that are not necessarily identifying almost invariably signals the familiar referent introducing function (p. 189).

[23] * Heim ends up interpreting the sequence 'A man greeted a woman. The woman dropped her umbrella' in the way traditional semantic theories would interpret 'A man greeted a woman who dropped her umbrella.'

[24] * The theory can be extended to cover quantification. When filing the sentence 'Every man laughed' one introduces a new file-card with the condition 'is a man' and tentatively updates this card with the condition 'laughed'. The sentence is true relative to the previous file just in case *every* tentative update results in a true file. And so on. For details of how this type of theory can deal with the interpretation of sentences containing generalized quantifiers, plurals, tense markers and anaphora, see Kamp and Reyle (1993) and Van Eijck and Kamp (1997).

128   *Problems of Compositionality*

interpretation is linked to the interpretation of an antecedent expression. In our example, the definite description 'the woman' and its antecedent 'a woman' are associated with the same file-card, which ensures that they are satisfied by the same individuals.[25]

4. REPLIES TO DONNELLAN'S OBJECTION

Russellian replies to Donnellan follow a three-step strategy. First, the Russellian acknowledges that the truth conditions in some cases do not seem to be Russellian, but maintains that (T_d^*) is correct anyway. Second, a semantics/pragmatics distinction is drawn. The Russellian offers a *pragmatic* explanation for the illusion of non-Russellian truth conditions, and argues that the non-Russellian is appealing to *semantic* ambiguity. Finally, the Russellian offers certain methodological considerations that tell against the semantic ambiguity thesis and in favor of the pragmatic explanation.[26]

Kripke (1977) discusses a Russellian reply motivated by ideas from Grice (1967) according to which although descriptions themselves do not refer to particular individuals, the speaker using descriptions may. In determining what a speaker refers to on a given occasion, we have to take into account both the meanings of the words she used and her intentions. A speaker may refer to something using words that do not refer to that thing if the situation is such that her audience is able to identify the speaker's referent using some conventional or *ad hoc* method. According to the Russellian the intuitive judgments cited by the either-or theorists are the result of a pragmatic illusion that emerges because we fail to distinguish between what the speaker means and what her words mean. The confusion is natural, since these normally coincide. The Russellian claims that it is possible to give a pragmatic

---

[25] There is an interesting suggestion in §19 of the Introduction to Berkeley's *Principles* concerning the interpretation of names that resembles Heim's idea: "... in reading and discoursing, names being for the most part used as letters in *algebra*, in which thought a particular quantity be marked by each letter, yet to proceed right it is not requisite that in every step each letter suggest to your thoughts, that particular quantity it was appointed to stand for." (Berkeley (1710), p. 17) In order to understand the equation '$x^2-4x+4=0$' I do not have to know which number 'x' stands for. However, I have to understand that in each step towards the solution, the letter 'x' will stand for the same number, namely the solution of the equation. So, in a certain sense 'x' is a coreferential expression in the derivation.

[26] * Arguments which more or less fit this schema can be found in Kripke (1977), Bach (1987), Neale (1990), Heim (1991), Ludlow and Neale (1991), and Salmon (1991).

Descriptions in Context 129

theory based on quantificational truth conditions that explains the range of phenomena mentioned by Donnellan. If this is correct, a decision has to be made between a pragmatically extended quantificational theory and an ambiguity theory with the same empirical explanatory power.[27]

There are methodological reasons to prefer a quantificational theory over a semantic ambiguity theory. Certainly, positing ambiguities is not an attractive move. More importantly, Kripke argues that the semantic ambiguity theorist needs the resources of her Russellian opponent to explain related phenomena anyway. Suppose a speaker from a distance mistakes Smith for Jones and utters the sentence 'Jones is raking the leaves'. What she meant to say is that Smith is raking the leaves, but her sentence did not mean this. She referred to Smith, although the name 'Jones' certainly does not refer to Smith. Furthermore, if the hearer realizes that the speaker mistook Smith for Jones, she will be able to see that by the utterance of the sentence the speaker intended to express the proposition that Smith is raking the leaves. The pragmatic principles she used to figure this out can account for Donnellan's referential uses of definite descriptions as well.[28]

---

[27] Donnellan (1966) states explicitly that he is not suggesting that sentences containing definite descriptions are either syntactically or semantically ambiguous. Later in Donnellan (1978), he repeats that he does not think that his distinction between the referential and the attributive uses of definite descriptions forces him to accept such an ambiguity. Kripke (1977) claims that Donnellan is inconsistent at this point. He says that "if the sentence is *not* (syntactically or) semantically ambiguous, it has only *one* analysis; to say that it has two distinct analyses is to attribute a syntactic or semantic ambiguity to it" (p. 255). This is less than obvious. Kripke's opinion is that the *use* of the sentence is pragmatically ambiguous, but that the sentence itself has only one analysis. Stalnaker (1972) has offered an alternative way to look at Donnellan's distinction. According to him, we can say that the sentences themselves may be pragmatically ambiguous in the sense that they express different propositions on different occasions, even if they have the same logical form. This view is in many ways similar to the one I will try to defend in section 6 of the present chapter.

[28] * There are two other standard methodological considerations but I fear they are not particularly strong. The first is that if the definite article is ambiguous in English, we should expect—contrary to fact—that there are other languages where the different senses are associated with different lexical items. The second is that we can see how referential use of definite descriptions would emerge even in a language where the definite article is postulated to be Russellian, and so, believing in semantic ambiguity seems gratuitous. The first argument assumes that semantic ambiguities must be accidental features of particular languages. The second argument neglects the fact that multiplicity of standard usage is an excellent *prima facie* reason for accepting multiplicity of meaning. (This latter point was emphasized by Reimer (1998b).)

130
Problems of Compositionality

5. REPLIES TO HEIM'S OBJECTION

Heim's objection to the quantificational view is that definite descriptions have no semantic uniqueness implications, and that this is in conflict with (T_d^*). Her theory departs radically from more conventional accounts, and this can be justified only if the Russellian answers to her objection turn out to be untenable. I think there are empirical and methodological reasons to think that this *is* the case. In this section I will focus on the empirical problems with the Russellian replies; in the next I will present the methodological points.

Kripke's defense of the Russellian theory against Donnellan rests on a distinction between what a speaker means when uttering her words on a given occasion and what her words mean on that occasion. This move does not help to explain the lack of uniqueness implications. It seems that when I utter (1) in a room that contains just one table I do not claim that there is just one thing such that it is a table.[29]

(1) The table is covered with books.

Moreover, this does not seem to be just a matter of what *I* mean when I utter those words, rather, a matter of what *my words* mean on a given occasion.

Of course, one might challenge this intuition, but such a challenge has serious consequences. One has to adopt the view according to which when I say 'The table is covered with books', strictly speaking I am *always* making a false claim, but since the falsity of my claim is obvious, my hearer will apply some principle of charity in her attempt to understand what I meant. Since failure of the uniqueness clause is quite ubiquitous in everyday discourse, a proponent of such a theory has to hold quite a peculiar view about communication according to which (i) sentences containing definite descriptions are *normally* used to express false propositions, and (ii) in order to understand such a sentence it is *normally* not enough to know what was said. I think neither of these claims is attractive.[30]

---

[29] This example, and the first attempt to criticize the Russellian theory on the account of uniqueness implications are from Strawson (1950), p. 225.

[30] An opposing view is presented in Bach (1987). Bach argues that there are many sentences containing definite descriptions that are *standardly* used S-non-literally. (p. 104) (A use of a sentence is S-non-literal when it is non-literal despite the fact that all

Descriptions in Context   *131*

The standard explanation of why a sentence like (1) seems to have no uniqueness implication is that the definite description in it is *incomplete*, in the sense in which this expression was introduced in the previous chapter. Deviation from the Russellian truth conditions is explained by the fact that the domain of quantification in (1) has to be restricted. So the logical form of (1) contains a contextually specifiable parameter whose value restricts the domain over which the quantification expressed by 'the' is to be interpreted.

There is some empirical evidence for this move. In natural languages the domain of quantification is often left unspecified. When someone says that 'All the tables are covered with books', this does not mean that all the tables in the universe are covered with books, only that all the tables in some relevant domain (e.g. the tables in this room) are covered with books. Similarly, when someone says that 'The table is covered with books', this means that the unique table in some relevant domain is covered with books. So, if I utter (1) in a room that has a single table, according to this approach the hearer who understands my utterance must recognize that the domain of quantification is contextually restricted to the objects in the room. Russellians pursuing this kind of explanation concede that context plays a double role in interpretation. It is used to determine what the speaker *meant* by using a certain expression, and also to determine what the speaker *said* by using those words on the given occasion.

This Russellian reply faces serious empirical difficulties, among which I will mention two. First, the context-dependency of definite descriptions seems to be different from the context-dependency of quantifier phrases. Consider the following minimal pair:

(2) A strange man was walking in the park. The man was wearing a hat.

(3) A strange man was walking in the park. Every man was wearing a hat.

The second sentence in (2) is naturally interpreted as 'The strange man who was walking in the park was wearing a hat', whereas 'Every

---

constituents of the sentence are used literally.) In these cases knowing the proposition expressed by the sentence is not enough for understanding the sentence.

132   *Problems of Compositionality*

strange man who was walking in the park was wearing a hat' is not a natural interpretation of the second sentence in (3). (3) should rather be interpreted as 'Every man who was walking in the park was wearing a hat'. The same holds for other quantifiers, like 'many', 'almost all', 'most', 'seven', etc. This example shows that adjectives in the previous discourse tend to influence the interpretation of definite descriptions, but not the interpretation of determiners that are clearly quantifiers. On the Russellian view this is peculiar: the mechanism of domain restriction for the definite articles seems to differ from the mechanism of domain restriction for other quantifiers.[31]

Another illustration of the difference between the context-dependency of quantifier phrases and descriptions is given in Reimer (1992). According to the quantificational theory in a *fixed* context, (1) and its Russellian expansion 'There is exactly one table and whatever is a table is covered with books' have to express the same proposition. Suppose the situation in which these sentences are uttered is the following. Two people are in an apartment where all the bookshelves are empty. There are two tables, one of them is covered with books, the other is empty. One of the people—apparently not noticing the table with books—asks the other why she has no books. If she responds by saying 'The table is covered with books', she expressed a true proposition. However, if she says 'There is exactly one table and whatever is a table is covered with books' she says something false. So it seems that whatever the contextually determined domain might be in this situation, if it is the same for (1) and its Russellian expansion, then they do not express the same proposition.

The second argument against the domain restriction view of the context-dependency of definite descriptions concerns cross-sentential anaphoric connections. Consider the following pair of sentences:[32]

---

[31] One might think that the problem is that 'the man' is singular. Notice, however, that the phenomenon is the same with the plural form of definite description:

    (i) Some strange men were walking in the park. The men were wearing hats.

    (i′) Some strange men were walking in the park. All men were wearing hats.

The reading of the second sequence according to which all *strange* men in the park were wearing hats is not impossible, but it is less natural than the one according to which all men walking in the park were wearing hats. Davies (1981) mentions the following minimal pair to make a related point (p. 162).

    (ii) I met some linguists. The linguists were educated in California.

    (ii′) I met some linguists. Most linguists were educated in California.

[32] * Other standard examples that can be used to make a similar point include 'The dog got in a fight with another dog' and 'If a bishop meets another bishop, the bishop blesses

Descriptions in Context

133

(4) A man was walking in the park. The man saw another man who was also walking in the park.

The sequence seems to be perfectly fine, but according to a straightforward application of the domain restriction view, it is a contradiction. The domain of quantification in the second sentence seems to be the set of walking men in the park, and so the sentence entails that there is exactly one man walking in the park. However, the sentence also entails that there are at least two men walking there.

So the domain of quantification in the second sentence has to be something else. But it is not clear what it could be. (4) can be uttered and understood in a context where nothing further is known about the man in the park mentioned by the first sentence. One might think that the domain can be specified as containing only the man mentioned in the first sentence. But this will not do. According to the quantificational theory, the first sentence of (4) expresses a general proposition, so it does not mention any man in particular. Alternatively, the advocate of the domain restriction view might suggest that the domain is specified by the intentions of the speaker. The second sentence quantifies over men in the park to whom the speaker intended to refer. This suggestion does not work either: the speaker may have had nobody in particular in mind when she uttered (4), but this does not prevent (4) from being meaningful and interpretable.

Realizing that there is no reasonable candidate for the domain of quantification in (4) that would render the sequence non-contradictory, someone might bite the bullet and claim that despite appearances (4) is in fact a contradiction. The hearer who is faced with this contradiction *reinterprets* (4) as saying something else, e.g. (5).

(5) A man who was walking in the park saw another man who was also walking in the park.

The consequence of such a position is a view according to which it is a very normal phenomenon that subsequent sentences force the addressee to reinterpret many of the previously interpreted sentences. It is certainly true that occasionally the hearer will have to do such a

---

the other bishop.' The former is from McCawley (1979), the latter is folklore (due, I think, originally to Hans Kamp).

134   *Problems of Compositionality*

reinterpretation. But, intuitively, these cases mark a certain *error* committed by at least one of the participants of the conversation. It seems quite misleading to say that the process of interpreting (4) resembles the process of interpreting (6):

(6) A man was walking in the park. Exactly one man was walking in the park and there is another man whom he saw walking in the park.

The cooperative hearer when she tries to make sense of the blatant contradiction in (6) will use the principle of charity and she will assume that the speaker *meant* something like that there was exactly one pair of men who accompanied each other. No such thing seems to be going on when one interprets (4).

To sum up, I think the lack of uniqueness implications remains a significant difficulty for the Russellian theories, even if we accept the fact that context may contribute to the specification of the domain.

6. METHODOLOGICAL CONSIDERATIONS

In this section, I will argue that essentially the same methodological considerations that supported the Russellian theory against Donnellan's objection favor a modified version of Heim's theory against the Russellian analysis.

One of the disadvantages of Heim's theory is that it postulates two new principles to provide an interpretation for descriptions. The Russellian theory uses the general mechanism of domain restriction that applies to the interpretation of other expressions as well. If we assume, for the sake of argument, that future Russellians will answer the empirical objections mentioned in the previous section, their account seems to be preferable on the grounds of parsimony.

However, Heim's is not the only possible coreferential theory. Let me suggest a slightly different one, which I will call *pragmatic* coreference theory (PCT). PCT departs from Heim's account in two crucial respects. First, it extends to *all* singular terms, and second, it changes the status of the Novelty and Familiarity Principles. The extension of the theory is fairly straightforward: proper names, demonstratives, anaphoric pronouns etc. are all associated with file-cards, and they are subject to the Familiarity Principle, just like definite

Descriptions in Context

descriptions. So, for example, when interpreting an utterance of the sentence 'John was smiling', the hearer has to find an old file-card with the condition 'is John' on it, and update that card with the condition 'was smiling'. According to the definitions of satisfaction and truth-for-a-file, the sentence cannot be true unless the file-card associated with the name 'John' is assigned some object who is John and who was smiling.[33]

The change of the status of the Novelty and Familiarity Principles amounts to the following. According to PCT these principles are not semantic rules that are always applied when a singular term is interpreted, but pragmatic maxims that can be violated due to contextual factors. For example, suppose I am telling a story to Alex about some strange man in the park. After a couple of sentences Bert joins us, and he wants to know what I was talking about. So I start again, using the indefinite description 'a man'. The Novelty Principle would require that Alex introduces a new file-card at this point, but that would clearly be a mistake. It is obvious that I am not talking about some other man in the park, I am merely repeating myself. Violations of the Familiarity Principle are even more common. I can simply start to talk to someone about the president of Tadjikistan, even if she does not know that Tadjikistan is an independent country, let alone that it has a president. She will simply introduce a new file-card for my definite description 'the president of Tadjikistan' and update it according to what I say.[34]

---

[33] From the facts that all singular terms are associated with file-cards and that definite descriptions, proper names, and demonstratives are subject to the Familiarity Principle, it does not follow that the coreferential theory is committed to the thesis that all singular terms behave the same as far as their semantics is concerned. In particular, one can account for the intuition that proper names and demonstratives are rigid designators. One technical device that can be used for this purpose is the so-called *external anchor* (Cf. Kamp and Reyle (1993), p. 248; Asher (1993), p. 82). An external anchor for a file-card 'n' is a function that maps the file-card onto some individual. The significance of the external anchor is that it constrains the possible embeddings of the file into the model. Thus any model in which the given file is true has to be such that the conditions associated with 'n' hold of the individual assigned to 'n' via the external anchor.

[34] * Turning the Novelty and Familiarity Principles into pragmatic rules of thumb has severe consequences for a Heim-style theory. I believe now that principles that can be overridden have no place in semantics. Not that semantic interpretation is free of defeasible reasoning—far from it. We use such reasoning in deciding whether a particular occurrence of 'bank' means the edge of a river or a financial institution, whether a particular occurrence of 'this' refers to the object the speaker is pointing to or the object she is looking at, or whether 'every' takes wide or narrow scope in the sentence 'Every

136   *Problems of Compositionality*

The most important consequence of these modifications is that in PCT, the same definite description can be a referring, quantifying or coreferring phrase depending on the context of utterance. Consider the sentence 'The man is in a good mood'. If this sentence is uttered in a normal context immediately after an utterance of 'John is smiling', its truth or falsity depends on the properties of John, so the definite description 'the man' is a referring phrase. If the sentence 'The man is in a good mood' is uttered in a normal context at the beginning of a conversation, the interpreter cannot find a suitable old file-card. In this case the Familiarity Principle is violated, and the hearer will assume that the speaker uses the sentence to achieve some stylistic effect. (For example, she wants to implicate that her story starts *in medias res*.) The hearer has to introduce a new file-card for the definite description 'the man', so the sentence is true if and only if the set of men in a good mood is not empty. In this case the description is a quantifying phrase. Finally, if the sentence 'The man is in a good mood' is uttered in a normal context after an utterance of 'A man was smiling', the definite description 'the man' cannot be either a referring or a quantifying phrase.

Another feature of PCT is that since the Novelty and the Familiarity Principles are regarded as pragmatic, they can be used in explaining various implicatures. According to the Familiarity Principle, the use of the definite description in an utterance of 'The table is covered with books' suggests that the condition 'is covered with books' be used to update a previously introduced file-card. However, if the context contains more than one table, the speaker cannot reasonably expect the hearer to be able to find the appropriate file-card. Consequently, even if the hearer is in doubt about the identity of the relevant table, she knows that according to the speaker the context contains a unique one. (Otherwise the speaker would have spoken misleadingly.) So, at least in this simple case, a pragmatic explanation along Gricean lines can be given for the *illusion* that by uttering this

---

child likes most animals' as it is used on a particular occasion. But these are all examples where due to our lack of contextual information, we either don't know which semantic rule to apply or we don't know how to apply it. Once we do know these things, the application of a semantic rule is automatic. I take this to be an essential feature of semantic rules. Although I call the Novelty and Familiarity Principles 'pragmatic' I still envision in this dissertation a semantic interpretation that relies on them. I now think this is a mistake. This consideration played an essential part in my abandonment of PCT in favor of the theory I advocate in 'Descriptions and Uniqueness'.

Descriptions in Context

sentence the speaker has *said* that there is a unique table covered with books. The pragmatic coreference theorist predicts that all uniqueness implications can be explained roughly in this manner.[35,36]

This Gricean explanation is quite similar to the one applied in the Russellian reply to Donnellan's objection. That was a pragmatic explanation for the illusion of non-Russellian truth conditions in the case of misidentification, this is a pragmatic explanation of the illusion of Russellian truth conditions in the case of definite descriptions without appropriate contextual antecedents. The analogy goes even further. A Kripke-style example can be used to show that PCT surpasses its quantificational rivals in terms of theoretical parsimony.

Suppose the speaker and the hearer know two people who have the name 'Jones'. Both of them are equally salient in a situation, i.e. there is no reason for the hearer to suppose that when the speaker utters (7) she means one, rather than the other.

(7) I met Jones yesterday.

In this case it is inappropriate for the speaker to utter (7), since the hearer will probably not be able to figure out which Jones is referred to. But once it is made clear which of the two people the speaker is talking about, she can use the name 'Jones' to refer to that person unambiguously.

(8) You know Jones the pianist? Well, I met Jones yesterday.

---

[35] Récanati (1989) states a minimalist principle in the following form: "A pragmatically determined aspect of meaning is part of what is said if and only if its determination is necessary for the utterance to express a complete proposition" (p. 101.) The quantificational and the coreferential theories agree that the uniqueness implication associated with a definite description in an utterance is a pragmatically determined aspect of meaning, but they disagree about the nature of this pragmatic determination. Most quantification theorists say that the uniqueness implication is a matter of implicit or explicit domain restriction, i.e. it is part of what is said. According to the coreferential theory, the uniqueness implication can be explained via general conversational maxims, i.e. it is not part of what is said by an utterance. The minimalist principle favors the coreferential approach.

[36] * In 'Descriptions and Uniqueness' I defend a version of the quantificational theory that is like PCT, insofar as it does not regard the uniqueness implications as part of what is said. There I give a more detailed derivation of how pragmatic uniqueness implications arise.

138 *Problems of Compositionality*

The explanation of this phenomenon is presumably that the hearer can assume that if the speaker uses an ambiguous name in a context, she will continue to refer to the same individual whenever she uses the name in the same discourse, unless she indicates the contrary. This case can be covered by the Familiarity Principle: names, like definite descriptions, tend to pick out a file-card that is already present in the context. (In other words, a speaker is normally not entitled to use names that are not known by the hearer without appropriate introduction.) Unless a radically different explanation can be given, the quantificational theory also needs a pragmatic principle like the Familiarity Principle to account for this phenomenon.

The Novelty Principle—or something quite similar to it—is also indispensable for the Russellian theorist. Grice noticed that expressions like 'a woman', 'a house', 'a college' etc. usually imply that the woman, the house or the college in question is not one's own wife, home or college.[37] Of course, this has nothing to do with the particular indefinites Grice mentioned. In a normal discourse, 'an F' usually does not indicate an F with which the speaker is intimately connected. However, the phenomenon is even more prevalent.

(9) Phillip and Morris were sitting in the non-smoking compartment of the train. A man suddenly lit a cigar and blew the smoke into Morris's face.

This sequence of sentences obviously suggests that the man who lit the cigar and blew the smoke into Morris's face was not Phillip. In normal contexts, the expression 'a man' is not appropriately used if the man in question was already mentioned, or was salient for some other reason. Such an explanation can be given using the Novelty Principle. 'A man' in (9) introduces a new file-card. Of course, when we check whether (9) is true, it may turn out that the only way to satisfy the file of (9) is to assign the same individual to the file-card associated with 'Phillip' and with the indefinite description 'a man'. In this case (9) would be still true, i.e. nothing that is said by (9) excludes the possibility that it was Phillip who blew the smoke into Morris's face. But the fact that the speaker used an indefinite description, and thereby instructed the hearer to introduce a new file-card for a man who blew the smoke into

---

[37] Grice (1967), pp. 37–8.

Descriptions in Context   *139*

Morris's face justifies a pragmatic implication that the speaker does not think that this person was Phillip. Otherwise, she would have spoken misleadingly; she would have said less than she was reasonably expected to, and would hereby have violated Grice's maxim of quantity. Again, unless a very different sort of explanation can be given here, the quantificational theory also needs something like the Novelty Principle for pragmatic explanations.[38]

Finally, let me mention a further consideration that speaks for PCT. This theory treats the uniqueness implications of definite descriptions and the non-uniqueness implications of indefinite descriptions on the same level. Consider the following example. A teacher wants to test whether her students remember that Newton and Leibniz independently invented the calculus. She might ask one of (10), (11) or (12).

(10) Who is an inventor of the calculus?

(11) Who is the inventor of the calculus?

(12) Who invented the calculus?

(10) is inappropriate, because the occurrence of the indefinite article gives away part of the answer, and (11) is misleading, because the occurrence of the definite article suggests that there is a unique person who invented the calculus. The teacher should avoid both articles, and simply ask (12). Importantly, (10) and (11) are inappropriate in a parallel manner, a fact which is well explained by PCT.[39] Quantificational theories, however, are committed to the implausible claim

---

[38] There are closely related phenomena that can be treated without invoking the Novelty Principle. Heim (1991) proposes the following principle: whenever in a context it is already known that the presupposition for the use of [the ζ] ξ is fulfilled, it is not allowed to use [a ζ] ξ instead (p. 515). Heim justifies this principle on the basis of the Gricean maxim of quantity. Unfortunately, the technique is not applicable in the case of (9): the hearer cannot infer anything from the fact that the speaker used an indefinite instead of a definite description in the second sentence, since in the context created by the interpretation of the first sentence the uniqueness presupposition of the definite description 'the man' is *not* fulfilled.

[39] * The indication of (10) that there is a unique inventor of the calculus seems no stronger than the indication of (11) that more than one person can claim that title. Continuing (10) with (10′) is just as awkward as continuing (11) with (11′):

  (8′) I don't mean to suggest that exactly one person invented the calculus.

  (9′) I don't mean to suggest that more than one person invented the calculus.

Whatever the correct semantics and pragmatics of questions, it seems clearly desirable that one be able to give very similar accounts of the inappropriateness of (10) and (11).

140 *Problems of Compositionality*

that the non-uniqueness implication in (10) is merely pragmatic, while the uniqueness implication in (11) is a matter of semantics.

7. COREFERRING PHRASES AND FILE-CARDS

Despite the empirical and the methodological advantages, the pragmatic coreferential theory will not be accepted as an adequate account of descriptions unless its conceptual foundation can be strengthened. In this section, I will try to clarify the nature of coreferring phrases by comparing them with referring and quantifying phrases, and I will say something about the question of what file-cards are supposed to be.

Referring phrases are object-dependent in the sense that the truth or falsity of a sentence containing such expressions depends on the properties of a particular object. In order to understand such a sentence, the hearer has to be able to identify this object. This is a fundamental principle concerning referring expressions, called—following Evans (1982)—*Russell's Principle*. As Evans points out, there is no question that the principle is true; the difficulty is to understand what it says. More precisely, it is clear that someone who understands a sentence containing a referring expression must be able to identify the referent in some sense; the problem is what exactly this ability amounts to. Whatever the correct analysis is, the understanding of referring phrases implies some sort of *identification* of a particular object.

By contrast, the understanding of sentences containing only quantifying phrases as nominal constituents does not involve identification. In order to understand such a sentence, one does not have to know who is who in the world, it is enough to be informed about the cardinality of certain sets of objects. Quantifiers are logical determiners in the sense of Mostowski (1957): they do "not allow us to distinguish between different elements of [the universe.]" [40]

Understanding of a sentence containing a definite description does not require the identification of a specific object, but it is not entirely free from all identification. Strawson (1959) introduced a contrast between two notions of identification. The first one is the identification of a particular, that to which the speaker refers. The second is what Strawson calls *story-relative identification*.

---

[40] Mostowski (1957), p. 13.

Descriptions in Context

> Consider ... the following case. A speaker tells a story which he claims to be factual. It begins: 'A man and a boy were standing at the fountain', and it continues: 'The man had a drink'. Shall we say that the hearer knows which or what particular is being referred to by the subject-expression in the second sentence? We might say so. For, of a certain range of two particulars, the words 'the man' serve to distinguish the one being referred to, by means of a description which applies only to him. [...] the hearer, hearing the second sentence, knows *which* particular creature is being referred to *of the two particular creatures being talked about by the speaker*; but he does not, without this qualification, know what particular creature is being referred to. The identification is within a certain story told by a certain speaker. It is identification within this story; but not identification within history.[41]

Strawson's story-relative identification is quite close to the identification of file-cards. According to the Familiarity Principle, in order to interpret such a sentence the hearer has to be able to identify a file-card that was previously introduced. Contra the quantificational theory, the coreferential view is committed to the claim that if the hearer in Strawson's example does not know that 'a man' and 'the man' *corefer* (in the sense that some man was standing at the fountain and the *very same man* had a drink) she does not understand the sentence. This is expressed by the claim that understanding those two sentences involves a certain kind of identification, though not the identification of a particular man.[42]

There is another way to contrast coreferring phrases with referring and quantificational ones. In a certain sense, both referring and quantifying phrases are *uneliminable*. A language without devices of reference would not be capable of expressing object-dependent propositions. If we assume that the domain of discourse is infinite, a language without devices of quantification cannot express certain

---

[41] Strawson (1959), p. 18.

[42] One might try to turn these considerations about identification into an argument against the quantificational view. There are two problems here. First, in order to make such an argument one has to be committed to the thesis that what we have to grasp in order to understand an expression is its meaning. (Cf. the discussion in section 2 of chapter 4.) Second, one has to show that story-relative identification is *not* identification of sets of individuals that can serve as domains of quantification.

142   *Problems of Compositionality*

quantitative relations among sets of objects. On the other hand, devices of cross-sentential coreference are in principle dispensable. According to PCT, the logical form of a sequence of sentences containing descriptions is always truth conditionally equivalent to some formula in standard logical notation. For example Strawson's example quoted above is equivalent to (13):

(13) $\exists x \exists y$ (man(x) $\wedge$ boy(y) $\wedge$ was-standing-at-the-fountain(x) $\wedge$ was-standing-at-the-fountain(y) $\wedge$ had-a-drink(x))

(Of course, I do not say that (13) *is* the logical form of Strawson's sentences. The language of logical forms, according to PCT, is a language with file-cards and conditions, not a language with variables and quantifiers.) Descriptions are convenient in constructing texts, but they are in no sense essential from the point of view of the expressive power of a language. So the coreferential theory of description is compatible with Quine's reading of Russell's theory. File-cards—at least in some sense—are eliminable from a language. As (13) shows, they can be replaced by bound variables. The difference between the Russellian position and the PCT concerns the nature of this elimination. According to the quantificational view, this can be done sentence by sentence; according to the coreferential theory, the elimination works only holistically, for a larger unit of the text.

If PCT is correct, we have to rethink the connection between the syntactic and the semantic notion of a sentence. There are many examples when syntactically well-formed sentences have no clear truth conditions, but it is generally assumed that they always have at least unclear truth conditions. Now, the second sentence in Strawson's example ('The man had a drink') is syntactically well-formed and perfectly understandable, but by itself has no truth conditions. We can assign truth conditions to the first sentence, or to the two together, but not to the second alone. It seems that context can play a peculiar role in the interpretation of a text: among other things it can determine which units of a text express propositions.

This might be considered a negative feature of PCT: unlike the Russellian theory that maintains a close connection between the syntactic and semantic notions of a sentence, the PCT can only accept a lax correlation. Note, however, that the situation is reversed with regard

Descriptions in Context 143

to singular terms. According to PCT, proper names, descriptions and pronouns all fall into the same semantic category; according to the Russellian theory proper names are referring expressions, descriptions belong among the quantificational phrases, and pronouns are sometimes devices of reference, sometimes devices of quantification, and sometimes devices of coreference.[43]

Let me turn now to the problem of file-cards. The coreferential theory spells out what is it for a file (a collection of file-cards) to be satisfied by a sequence of individuals and what is it for a file to be true; it also describes how we can use files as a level of semantic representation for sentences. Thus it shows the notion of file-card to be useful. But while usefulness lends a certain legitimacy to notions, it does not make them more intelligible.

A realist explication of the notion of files is tempting: one can take the semantic representations to be psychological entities. The idea that mental representations associated with singular terms are similar to file-cards was already suggested in Lockwood (1971). According to Lockwood, when interpreting an identity statement the hearer has to merge two 'mental files' that were already present in her mind. Zeevat (1989) argues that the entities that have to be identified when one interprets a definite description are concepts in the mind. They are organized in a logical structure that reflects the syntactic structure of the sentence; these complexes are called thoughts. Truth is defined in terms of thoughts: a thought is true iff it can be mapped in a structure-preserving way to a fact in reality.

Zeevat calls his concepts intentions, and takes them to be psychological entities of some sort. I will mention two objections to such a view. First, if files are intentions, then in order to interpret a definite description one has to identify intentions that the speaker has. However, in many cases there is no specific thing that the speaker has in mind. If the speaker says 'A man killed Jones', she may or may not have a particular person in mind, and may or may not intend to

---

[43] In Section 3 of Chapter 2, I introduced two basic principles of the theory of reference. The first was that genuine sentences are true or false, not both. The second was that if they contain a genuine singular term, their truth or falsity depends on the properties of a specific object. According to the Russellian theory, descriptions are not genuine singular terms, despite the fact that they are syntactically similar to, say, complex demonstratives. According to PCT, sentences containing descriptions may not be genuine sentences, despite the fact that they are syntactically similar to genuine sentences.

144   *Problems of Compositionality*

communicate something about that person. In any case, if the next sentence contains the description 'the murderer', the condition 'is a murderer' has to be written on the file-card associated with the indefinite description 'a man'. Second, we use file-cards to determine the truth conditions of sentences. But meanings, if they determine the truth conditions, relative to the way the world is, cannot be in the head. Consequently, one cannot identify a collection of file-cards with psychological states.[44]

There is an alternative instrumentalist explication of file-cards, based on Chapter II of Heim (1982). Here *variables* play the role of the file-cards. Both definite and indefinite descriptions are translated into the language of the semantic representation as variables that are bound by unselective quantifiers.[45] The theory introduced here yields more standard representations than the File-Change Semantics of Chapter III in Heim (1982), but the truth conditions of sentences containing descriptions are the same. (The logical forms are similar to the regimented formula in (13), except that they contain a single existential quantifier instead of a different one for each variable.) In this way, one could argue that file-cards *are* variables, and whatever else is suggested by the metaphor of the file clerk should not be taken very seriously.

There is nothing wrong with such an account as a theory in formal semantics, but it is not useful as an explication of the intuitive notion of a file-card. Maybe file-cards are variables, but they are certainly not the kind of variables that we are most familiar with. Variables in most formal languages receive their values via an assignment function during the process of interpreting the formula in which they occur. The interpretation of subsequent formulae cannot change or modify the value of a variable in a standard interpretation. Bound variables can be replaced uniformly by other bound variables without changing the truth conditions of the formula. But this is not the case in the formalism Heim suggests.

I think we need a middle position between the realist and the instrumentalist explications of file-cards. The semantic structure

---

[44] * The first of these objections is effective only against Zeevat's particular conception of what mental files are like. The second becomes ineffective if we assume that mental files play no semantic role. In my 'Descriptions and Uniqueness' I argue that files are mental representations.

[45] Unselective quantifiers simultaneously bind all variables in their scope. The idea was introduced in Lewis (1975a).

Descriptions in Context

revealed by the coreferential theory should be taken more seriously than a mere heuristic device, but it should not be regarded as the structure of thought. I would like to suggest that file-cards are *expressions* of a formal language which is used for presenting the logical form of natural language expressions. This means that I recommend the abandonment of the straightforward first-order formalism in the logical form, and use instead a formal language, like Heim's file system, or like Kamp's discourse representational language. File-cards (or discourse referents) are used in these languages in a way that is analogous to the use of *theoretical terms* in science. The reference of file-cards is fixed by the text itself, in much the way that theoretical terms have their interpretation fixed implicitly by an entire theory. The idea of holistic interpretation of theoretical terms is described very clearly in Lewis (1972).

Suppose a detective reconstructs a crime for the assembled people in the drawing room of a country house. The detective who does not know (or does not want to tell) who committed the crime uses imaginary names 'X', 'Y' and 'Z' in his story. In the beginning his audience knows nothing about the bearers of these names. They gradually gather information about them as the detective proceeds in telling the story. Lewis calls these terms *theoretical*, or *T*-terms. All other terms in the story have a previously fixed meaning. These are called *O*-terms by Lewis, where '*O*' stands for *other*, *old* or *original*. If there is a triple of individuals such that if one substitutes their names for 'X', 'Y' and 'Z', then we get a true story, the triple *realizes* the story. If there is exactly one such triple then the story is *uniquely* realized. If the story is not realized, i.e. if there are no individuals that occupy the roles set forth by the detective, then what he said is false.

One can take this example as a suggestion for the interpretation of descriptions in general. The detective could have used descriptions instead of the imaginary names. So, when he first mentioned that X is a sailor who returned from Alaska, he could have said instead 'a sailor who returned from Alaska', and later he could have referred to X as 'the sailor who returned from Alaska', or just as 'the sailor'.

The file-cards associated with descriptions can simply be regarded as *T*-terms in the language of logical forms. They are not psychological entities, but expressions whose meaning gets fixed by the story itself. In saying that the file-cards are *T*-terms, we maintain the view that they are entities that get introduced into a discourse and are associated with

146   *Problems of Compositionality*

semantic information. Moreover, as the processing of the text advances, the hearer may associate new pieces of information with the same *T*-term.[46] To the extent that we understand the notion of theoretical term, we also understand what file-cards are.[47]

8. SUMMARY

In this chapter, I discussed the semantics of descriptions. In Section 1, I hinted at a certain parallel between the Moorean line about adjectives, defended in the previous chapter and a Meinongean line about descriptions. In the rest of the chapter I argued for a revised Meinongean theory of description, according to which all singular terms belong to the same semantic category. In Section 2, I distinguished among four types of views about descriptions. I conceded that Russell's arguments against the *referential* view are correct. In Section 3, I presented two objections to the Russellian theory. In Section 4, I argued, following Kripke, that the first one (due to Donnellan) is not a serious challenge for the Russellian; in Section 5, I showed that the same arguments are not effective against the other objection (due to Heim). Furthermore, I argued that the problem of incomplete descriptions constitutes a serious empirical difficulty for the defender of the quantificational view. In Section 6, I presented a modified version of Heim's theory, and argued that the very same arguments Kripke used against Donnellan can be used by the defender of the modified theory against the Russellians. Finally, in Section 7, I

---

[46] In certain respects Landman (1986) presents a similar view on the nature of file-cards. He argues that file-cards are neither private psychological representations, nor variables in the logical form. File-cards are so-called *pegs*: "objects we assume in conversation, and which we follow through information growth. On very partial information they are indiscernible from other objects to which they may be identical, but also from which they may be discernible at the end" (p. 128). Pegs are the kind of things on which we can "hang" properties in a discourse. Though the analogy is suggestive, I think we have no solid conception of what these entities are supposed to be. (Landman says that the question 'Do pegs exist?' is not merely irrelevant, but also nonsensical.) The analogy between file-cards and theoretical terms seems to me to be easier to grasp.

[47] Lewis (1970a) and Lewis (1972) argue that the use of theoretical terms has a strong implicit uniqueness implication. If this implication is *pragmatic*, Lewis's claim is not in conflict with the idea that file-cards can be regarded as theoretical terms. If, however, the implication is supposed to be *semantic* (i.e. if the meaning of theoretical terms in a given theory is supposed to rule out their multiple realizability), file-cards cannot be theoretical terms. Lewis's commitment to unique realizability of theoretical terms was criticized recently in Bedard (1993).

Descriptions in Context 147

tried to clarify somewhat the notion of a coreferential phrase, and that of a file-card.

The moral of Chapters 4 and 5 is that neither the interpretation of context-sensitive adjectives, nor that of context-sensitive descriptions presents a serious difficulty for the defender of the context thesis. The strategy in both cases to say that in the logical form of these expressions there are certain parameters whose values are fixed by the context of utterance. However, in spelling out the details of these theories, one notices that the original simpler notion of context has to be replaced by more and more complicated ones. Context-sensitive adjectives give reason to believe that the meaning of certain expressions within an utterance may be part of the context that contributes to determining the meaning of other expressions within the *same* utterance (cf. Section 4, Chapter 4). Context-sensitive descriptions give reason to believe that context plays a role in determining whether a syntactically well-formed sentence expresses a proposition at all (cf. Section 5, Chapter 5).

CHAPTER 6

In Place of a Conclusion

The reader has no doubt realized that the central question of this dissertation, namely, whether the principle of compositionality is true, has remained unanswered. At the end of Chapter 2, I noted that the answer to this question is of some importance. A positive answer opens up a possibility of meeting Bloomfield's challenge: if the principle of compositonality—interpreted as a general claim about all possible human languages—is true, then linguistic semantics—an empirical theory based on the judgments of ordinary speakers—is possible. If the principle is false, then it is far from clear what to say about Bloomfield's challenge.

One can split the original question concerning the truth of compositionality into two related ones: 'Why are we inclined to believe in compositionality?' and 'Should we yield to the inclination?' In Chapters 3–5, I argued against *quick* answers to these questions.

The quick answer to the first question is that we are inclined to believe that languages are compositional because we are able to understand expressions we have never heard before, and this fact cannot be explained without the assumption that the meanings of these new expressions are determined by the meanings of their constituents and the way the constituents are combined. In Chapter 3, I argued that there are problems with this reasoning, and in the last section of that chapter, I indicated that perhaps our real intuitions are misdescribed here. What we are certain of is only that we understand new expressions by grasping some familiar features those expressions have, and recognizing that they fit into a familiar pattern. This shows only that languages are systematic, not that they are compositional.

149

150 *Problems of Compositionality*

The quick answer to the second question is that even though the principle of compositionality might be true, the pervasiveness of context-dependency in natural languages casts serious doubt on it. Several semanticists have suggested that the interpretation of adjectives and/or descriptions requires the loosening of the requirement of compositionality. In chapters 4 and 5, I argued that the context-dependency of most adjectives and descriptions is no real threat to compositionality. Furthermore, if one recognizes the presence of contextual parameters in the logical forms of adjectives and descriptions, it is possible to simplify the semantics of these expressions.

Like most of us, I believe that the principle of compositionality is true, but unlike many of us, I do not think that my belief is fully justified. I suspect, ultimately the question whether the principle is true will be decided on the basis of the success of semantic theories that are built on it. The real problem of compositionality is whether the context thesis is tenable, and the only way to know that is to see whether theories which locate context-sensitivity in accordance with it stand up to scrutiny.

Suppose everything turns out to be as we expected and the meanings of complex expressions in natural languages can indeed be characterized compositionally. Then we will have answered the second question: yes, we should yield to our inclination in accepting the principle of compositionality. Of course, by this we will not have answered the first question. If compositionality turns out to be true, it will seem even more puzzling: why did we have the inclination to believe in it *before* the real evidence came in? How is it that, even though we are exceedingly uncertain what meaning is, we are convinced that, whatever it is, the meaning of a complex expression supervenes on the meanings of its parts and on its structure?

Bibliography

Asher, N. (1993) *Reference to Abstract Objects in Discourse*. Dordrecht: Kluewer.

Bach, K. (1987) *Thought and Reference*. Oxford: Clarendon Press.

Barwise J. and Cooper J. (1981) 'Generalized Quantifiers and Natural Language.' *Linguistics and Philosophy* **4**, pp. 159–219.

Barwise J. and J. Perry (1983) *Situations and Attitudes*. Cambridge, MA: MIT Press.

Bedard, K. A. (1993) 'Partial Denotations of Theoretical Terms.' *Noûs* **27**, pp. 499–511.

Berkeley, G. (1710) *The Principles of Human Knowledge*. In C. M. Turbayne ed., *Principles, Dialogues, and Philosophical Correspondence*. Indianapolis: Bobbs-Merrill, 1965.

Bloomfield, L. (1933) *Language*. New York: Holt, Rinehart & Winston.

Burge, T. (1990) 'Frege on Sense and Linguistic Meaning.' In D. Bell and N. Cooper eds., *The Analytic Tradition*. Oxford: Basil Blackwell, pp. 30–60.

Cartwright, R. (1987) 'On the Origins of Russell's Theory of Descriptions.' In *Philosophical Essays*. Cambridge, MA: MIT Press, pp. 95–133.

Cappelen, H. and E. LePore (1997) 'Varieties of Quotation.' *Mind* **106**, pp. 429–50.

Chastain, C. (1975) 'Reference and Context.' In K. Gunderson ed., *Minnesota Studies in the Philosophy of Science. Vol. 7: Language, Mind, and Knowledge*. Minneapolis: University of Minnesota Press, pp. 194–269.

Chomsky, N. (1980) *Rules and Representations*. New York: Columbia University Press.

Cresswell, M. J. (1985) *Structured Meanings: The Semantics of Propositional Attitudes*. Cambridge, MA: MIT Press.

Crimmins, M. (1992) *Talk about Belief*. Cambridge, MA: MIT Press.

152   *Bibliography*

Davidson, D. (1965) 'Theories of Meaning and Learnable Languages.' In Y. Bar Hillel ed., *Logic, Methodology and Philosophy of Science*. Reprinted in D. Davidson *Inquiries into Truth and Interpretation*. Oxford: Clarendon Press, 1985, pp. 3–15.

Davidson, D. (1970) 'Semantics for Natural Languages.' In D. Davidson and G. Harman eds., Logic and Grammar. Reprinted in D. Davidson *Inquiries into Truth and Interpretation*. Oxford: Clarendon Press, 1985, pp. 55–64.

Davies, M. (1981) *Meaning, Quantification, Necessity*. London: Routledge.

Dekker, P. (1994) 'Predicate Logic with Anaphora.' In M. Harvey and L. Santelmann eds., *Proceedings from Semantics and Linguistic Theory IV*. Ithaca: Cornell University Department of Modern Languages and Linguistics: 79–95.

Donnellan, K. (1966) 'Reference and Definite Descriptions.' *Philosophical Review* **75**. Reprinted in A. P. Martinich ed., *The Philosophy of Language*. Oxford: Oxford University Press, 1985, pp. 236–48.

Donnellan, K. (1978) 'Speaker Reference, Descriptions, and Anaphora.' In P. Cole ed., *Syntax and Semantics, vol. 9*: Pragmatics. New York: Academic Press, pp. 47–68.

Dummett, M. (1973) *Frege. Philosophy of Language*. Cambridge, MA: Harvard University Press.

Dummett, M. (1989) 'More about Thoughts.' *Notre Dame Journal of Formal Logic* **30**. Reprinted in M. Dummett, *Frege and Other Philosophers*. Oxford: Clarendon Press, 1991, pp. 289–314.

Dummett, M. (1991) *The Logical Basis of Metaphysics*. Cambridge, MA: Harvard University Press.

van Eijk, J. and H. Kamp (1997) 'Representing Discourse in Context.' In J. van Benthem and A ter Meulen eds., *Handbook of Logic and Language*. Amsterdam: Elsevier and Cambridge, MA: MIT Press: 179–238.

Elugardo, R. (1999) 'Mixed Quotation.' In K. Murasugi and R. Stainton eds., *Philosophy and Linguistics*. Boulder, CO: Westview Press, 1999, pp. 223–44.

Evans G. (1976) 'Semantic Structure and Logical Form.' In G. Evans and J. McDowell eds., *Truth and Meaning: Essays in Semantics*. Reprinted in *Collected Papers*. Oxford: Clarendon Press, 1985, pp. 49–75.

Evans G. and J. McDowell (1976) 'Introduction.' In G. Evans and J. McDowell eds., *Truth and Meaning: Essays in Semantics*. Oxford: Clarendon Press, pp. vii—xxiii.

Evans, G. (1982) *The Varieties of Reference*. Oxford: Clarendon Press.

Bibliography

Field, H. (1972) 'Tarski's Theory of Truth.' *Journal of Philosophy* **69**, pp. 347–75.

Field, H. (1994) 'Deflationist Views of Meaning and Content.' *Mind* **103**, pp. 249–85.

Fine, K. (1989) 'The Problem of *De Re* Modality.' In J. Almog et al. ed., *Themes from Kaplan.* Oxford: Oxford University Press: 197–272.

Fodor, J. A. (1980) 'Methodological Solipsism Considered as a Research Strategy in Cognitive Psychology.' *The Behavioral and Brain Sciences* **3**. Reprinted in *Representations.* Cambridge, MA: MIT Press, 1983, pp. 225–53.

Fodor, J. D. and I. Sag (1982) 'Referential and Quantificational Indefinites.' *Linguistics and Philosophy* **5**, pp. 355–98.

Frawley, W. (1992) *Linguistic Semantics.* Hillside: Laurence Erlbaum Associates Publisher.

Frege, G. (1891) 'On the Law of Inertia.' *Zeitschrift für Philosophie und philosophische Kritik* **98**. Reprinted in B. McGuinness ed., *Collected Papers on Mathematics, Logic, and Philosophy.* Oxford: Basil Blackwell, 1984, pp. 123–36.

Frege, G. (1892) 'On Concept and Object.' *Vierteljahrschrift für wissenschaftliche Philosophie* **16**. Reprinted in B. McGuinness ed., *Collected Papers on Mathematics, Logic, and Philosophy.* Oxford: Basil Blackwell, 1984, pp. 182–94.

Frege, G. (1906a) 'Foundations of Geometry/II.' *Jahresbericht der Deutschen Mathemtiker-Vereinigung* **15**. Reprinted in B. McGuinness ed., *Collected Papers on Mathematics, Logic, and Philosophy.* Oxford: Basil Blackwell, 1984, pp. 293–340.

Frege, G. (1906b) 'Introduction to Logic.' In H. Hermes et al. eds., *Posthumous Writings.* Chicago: University of Chicago Press, 1979, pp. 185–96.

Frege, G. (1914) 'Logic in Mathematics.' In H. Hermes et al. eds., *Posthumous Writings.* Chicago: University of Chicago Press, 1979, pp. 201–50.

Frege, G. (1914?) 'Letter to Jourdain.' Originally undated. In G. Gabriel et al. eds., *Philosophical and Mathematical Correspondence.* Chicago: University of Chicago Press, 1980, pp. 78–80.

Frege, G. (1919) 'Notes for Ludwig Darmstaedter.' In H. Hermes et al. eds., *Posthumous Writings.* Chicago: University of Chicago Press, 1979, pp. 253–57.

Frege, G. (1923) 'Compound Thoughts.' Reprinted in B. McGuiness, ed., *Collected Papers on Mathematics, Logic, and Philosophy.* Oxford: Blackwell, 1984: 390–406.

154 Bibliography

Gamut, L. T. F. (1991) *Logic, Language, and Meaning*. Chicago: University of Chicago Press.

Geach, P. (1956) 'Good and Evil.' Reprinted in P. Foot ed., *Theories of Ethics*. Oxford: Oxford University Press, 1967, pp. 64–74.

Geach, P. (1965) 'Logical Procedures and the Identity of Expressions.' *Ratio* **7**. Reprinted in *Logic Matters*. Berkeley: University of California Press, 1972, pp. 108–14.

Grice, H. P. (1967) 'Logic and Conversation.' In P. Cole and J. Morgan eds., *Syntax and Semantics, vol. 3*. Reprinted in *Studies in the Way of Words*. Cambridge, MA: Harvard University Press, 1989. pp. 22–40.

Groenendijk, J. and M. Stokhoff (1991) 'Dynamic Predicate Logic.' *Linguistics and Philosophy* 14:39–100.

Heim, I. (1982) *The Semantics of Definite and Indefinite Noun Phrases*. Doctoral thesis, University of Massachusetts, Amherst.

Heim, I. (1983) 'File-Change Semantics and the Familiarity Theory of Definiteness.' In R. Bäuerle et al. eds., *Meaning, Use and Interpretation of Language*. Berlin: de Gruyter, pp. 164–90.

Heim, I. (1991) 'Artikel und Definitheit.' In A. v. Stechow and D. Wunderlich eds., Semantik: Ein Internationales Handbuch der zeitgenössischen Forschung. Berlin: de Gruyter, pp. 487–535.

Higginbotham, J. (1985), 'On Semantics.' *Linguistic Inquiry* **16**, pp. 547–93.

Hintikka, J. (1981) 'Theories of Truth and Learnable Languages.' In S. Kanger and S. Öhman eds., *Philosophy and Grammar*. Dordrecht: Reidel Publishing Company, pp. 37–58.

Hume, D. (1748) *Enquiry Concerning Human Understanding*. Edited by L. A. Selby-Bigge, revised edition by P. H. Nidditch. Oxford: Clarendon Press, 1975.

Jackendoff, R. (1983) *Semantics and Cognition*. Cambridge, MA: MIT Press.

Janssen, T. M. V. (1983) *Foundations and Applications of Montague Grammar*. Amsterdam: Mathematisch Centrum.

Janssen, T. M. V. (1997) 'Compositionality.' In J. Van Benthem and A. Ter Meulen eds., *Handbook of Logic and Language*. Amsterdam: Elsevier and Cambridge, MA: MIT Press: 417–473.

Kadmon, N. (1987) *On Unique and Non-Unique Reference and Asymmetric Quantification*. PhD. Dissertation, University of Massachusetts at Amherst. Garland Publishing Inc., 1992.

Kamp, H. (1975) 'Two Theories about Adjectives.' In E. L. Keenan ed., *Formal Semantics of Natural Language*. Cambridge: Cambridge University Press, pp. 123–56.

Bibliography

Kamp, H. (1981) 'A Theory of Truth and Semantic Interpretation.' In J. Groenendijk, et al. eds., *Formal Methods in the Study of Natural Language*. Amsterdam: Amsterdam Centre, pp. 277–322.

Kamp, H. and U. Reyle (1993) *From Discourse to Logic*. Dordrecht: Kluewer.

Kaplan, D. (1977) 'Demonstratives. An Essay on the Logic, Metaphysics, and Epistemology of Demonstratives and other Indexicals.' Circulated as a manuscript, reprinted in J. Perry and H. K. Wettstein eds., *Themes from Kaplan*. Oxford: Oxford University Press, 1989, pp. 481–563.

Karttunen, L. (1976) 'Discourse Referents.' In J. McCawley ed., *Syntax and Semantics, vol. 7: Notes from the Linguistic Underground*. New York: Academic Press, pp. 363–85.

Kazmi, A. and F. J. Pelletier (1998) 'Is Compositionality Vacuous?' *Linguistics and Philosophy* **21**: 629–633.

Keenan E. and D. Westerstahl (1997) 'Generalized Quantifiers in Linguistics and Logic.' In J. van Benthem and A. ter Meulen eds., *Handbook of Logic and Language*. Amsterdam: Elsevier, pp. 837–94.

Kim, J. (1984) 'Concepts of Supervenience.' *Philosophy and Phenomenological Research* **45**. Reprinted in *Supervenience and Mind*, Cambridge: Cambridge University Press, 1993, pp. 53–78.

Krámský, J. (1972) *The Article and the Concept of Definiteness in Language*. The Hague: Mouthon & Co.

Kripke, S. (1977) 'Speaker Reference and Semantic Reference.' In P. A. French et al. eds., *Contemporary Perspectives in the Philosophy of Language*. Reprinted in A. P. Martinich ed., *The Philosophy of Language*. Oxford: Oxford University Press, 1985, pp. 249–67.

Kripke, S. (1979) 'A Puzzle about Belief.' In A. Margalit ed., *Meaning and Use*. Dordrecht: Reidel: 239–83.

Kripke, S. (1980) *Naming and Necessity*. Oxford: Basil Blackwell.

Lakoff, G. (1988) 'Cognitive Semantics.' In U. Eco et al. eds., *Meaning and Mental Representation*. Bloomington, IN: Indiana University Press, pp. 119–54.

Landman, F. (1986) 'Pegs and Alecs.' In *Towards a Theory of Information*. Dordrecht: Foris, pp. 97–136.

Leibniz G. W. (1765) *New Essays on Human Understanding*. Cambridge: Cambridge University Press, 1981.

Lewis, D. (1970a) 'How to Define Theoretical Terms.' *Journal of Philosophy* **67**. Reprinted in *Philosophical Papers, vol. 1*. Oxford: Oxford University Press, 1986, pp. 78–95.

156 *Bibliography*

Lewis, D. (1970b) 'General Semantics.' *Synthese* **22**. Reprinted in *Philosophical Papers, vol. 1.* Oxford: Oxford University Press, 1986, pp. 189–229.

Lewis, D. (1972) 'Psychophysical and Theoretical Identifications.' *Australasian Journal of Philosophy* **50**, pp. 249–58.

Lewis, D. (1975a) 'Adverbs of Quantification.' In E. Keenan ed., *Formal Semantics of Natural Language.* Cambridge: Cambridge University Press, pp. 3–15.

Lewis, D. (1975b) 'Languages and Language.' In K. Gunderson ed., *Minnesota Studies in the Philosophy of Science, vol. 7.* Reprinted in *Philosophical Papers, vol. 1.* Oxford: Oxford University Press, 1986, pp. 163–88.

Lewis, D. (1979) 'Scorekeeping in a Language Game.' *Journal of Philosophical Logic* **8**. Reprinted in *Philosophical Papers, vol. 1.* Oxford: Oxford University Press, 1986, pp. 233–49.

Lockwood, M. (1971) 'Identity and Reference.' In M. K. Munitz ed., *Identity and Individuation.* New York: New York University Press, pp. 199–211.

Ludlow, P. and S. Neale (1991) 'Indefinite Descriptions: In Defense of Russell.' *Linguistics and Philosophy* **14**, pp. 171–202.

Martin, R. L. (1994) *The Meaning of Language.* Cambridge, MA: MIT Press.

McCawley, J. (1979) 'Presupposition and Discourse Structure.' In D. Dinneen and C. Oh eds., *Syntax and Semantics. Vol. 11.* New York: Academic Press, pp. 371–88.

Millikan, R. G. (1984) *Language, Thought, and Other Biological Categories.* Cambridge, MA: MIT Press.

Montague, R. (1970a) 'English as a Formal Language.' In B. Visentini et al. eds., Linguaggi nella Società e nella Tecnica. Reprinted in R. H. Thomason ed., *Formal Philosophy.* New Haven: Yale University Press, 1974, pp. 188–221.

Montague, R. (1970b) 'Universal Grammar.' *Theoria* **36**. Reprinted in R. H. Thomason ed., *Formal Philosophy.* New Haven: Yale University Press, 1974, pp. 222–46.

Moore, G. E. (1903), *Principia Ethica.* First paperback edition, second reprint, Cambridge: Cambridge University Press, 1962.

Moore, G. E. (1944?) 'Moore's Paradox.' Originally untitled and undated manuscript, reprinted in T. Baldwin ed., Selected Writings. London: Routledge, pp. 207–12.

Mostowski, A. (1957) 'On a Generalization of Quantifiers.' *Fundamenta Mathematicae* **44**, pp. 12–36.

Bibliography 157

Muskens, R. (1994) 'Compositional Discourse Representation Theory.' In P. Dekker and M. Stokhoff eds., *Proceedings of the Ninth Amsterdam Colloquium*. Amsterdam: ILLC: 467–86.

Neale, S. (1990) *Descriptions*. Cambridge, MA: MIT Press.

Nunberg G., I. A. Sag and T. Wasow (1994) 'Idioms.' *Language* **70**: 491–538.

Partee, B. (1984) 'Compositionality.' In F. Landman and F. Veltman eds., *Varieties of Formal Semantics*. Dordrecht: Foris: 281–312.

Pelletier, F. J. (1994) 'The Principle of Semantic Compositionality.' *Topoi* **13**: 11–24.

Pietroski, P. (1999) 'Compositional Quotation (without Parataxis).' In K. Murasugi and R. Stainton eds., *Philosophy and Linguistics*. Boulder, CO: Westview Press, 1999, pp. 245–58.

Pigden, C. R. (1990) 'Geach on 'Good'.' *The Philosophical Quarterly* **40**, No. 159., pp. 129–54.

Putnam, H. (1970) 'Is Semantics Possible?' In H. Kiefer and M. Munitz eds., *Languages, Belief, and Metaphysics*. Reprinted in *Mind, Language and Reality: Philosophical Papers, vol. 2*. Cambridge: Cambridge University Press, 1975, pp. 139–52.

Putnam, H. (1975) 'The Meaning of 'Meaning'.' In K. Gunderson ed., *Minnesota Studies in the Philosophy of Science, vol. 7*. Reprinted in *Mind, Language and Reality: Philosophical Papers, vol. 2*. Cambridge: Cambridge University Press, 1975, pp. 215–71.

Quine, W. V. O. (1948) 'On What There Is.' *Review Of Metaphysics* **2**. Reprinted in *From a Logical Point of View*. Cambridge, MA: Harvard University Press, 1953, pp. 1–20.

Quine, W. V. O. (1953) 'Mr. Strawson on Logical Theory.' *Mind* **62**. Reprinted in *The Ways of Paradox*. Cambridge, MA: Harvard University Press, 1966, pp. 137–57.

Quine, W. V. O. (1960) *Word and Object*. Cambridge, MA: MIT Press.

Quine W. V. O. (1967) 'Russell's Ontological Development.' *Journal of Philosophy* **63**. Reprinted in *Theories and Things*. Cambridge, MA: Harvard University Press, 1981, pp. 73–85.

Quine, W. V. O. (1978) 'Use and Its Place in Meaning.' *Erkenntnis* **13**. Reprinted in *Theories and Things*. Cambridge, MA: Harvard University Press, 1981, pp. 43–54.

Récanati, F. (1989) 'The Pragmatics of What Was Said.' *Mind and Language* **4**. Reprinted in S. Davis ed., *Pragmatics: A Reader*. Oxford: Oxford University Press, 1991, pp. 97–120.

Récanati, F. (1993) *Direct Reference*. Oxford: Blackwell.

158   *Bibliography*

Reimer, M. (1992) 'Incomplete Descriptions.' *Erkenntnis* **37**, pp. 347–63.

Reimer, M. (1998a) 'The Wettstein/Salmon Debate: Critique and Resolution.' *Pacific Philosophical Quarterly* **79**, pp. 130–51.

Reimer, M. (1998b) 'Donnellan's Distinction/Kripke's Test.' *Analysis* **58**, pp. 89–100.

Russell, B. (1903) *Principles of Mathematics*. New York: Norton & Co.

Russell, B. (1904) 'Letter to Frege.' Published in G. Gabriel et al. eds., G. Frege, *Philosophical and Mathematical Correspondence*. Chicago: University of Chicago Press, 1980, pp. 166–70.

Russell, B. (1905) 'On Denoting.' *Mind* **14**. Reprinted in R. C. Marsh ed., *Logic and Knowledge*. London: Unwin Hyman, 1956, pp. 39–56.

Salmon, N. (1989) 'Reference and Information Content: Names and Descriptions.' In D. Gabbay and F. Guenthner eds., *Handbook of Philosophical Logic. Vol. 4: Topics in the Philosophy of Language.* Dordrecht: Kluwer: 409–462.

Salmon, N. (1991) ''The Pragmatic Fallacy.' *Philosophical Studies* **63**, pp. 83–97.

Schiffer, S. (1987) *Remnants of Meaning*. Cambridge, MA: MIT Press.

Stainton, R. (1999) 'Remarks on the Syntax and Semantics of Mixed Quotation.' In K. Murasugi and R. Stainton eds., *Philosophy and Linguistics.* Boulder, CO: Westview Press, 1999, pp. 259–78.

Stalnaker, R. (1972) 'Pragmatics.' In D. Davidson and G. Harman eds., *Semantics of Natural Language*. Dordrecht: Reidel, pp. 380–97.

Stalnaker, R. (1974) 'Pragmatic Presuppositions.' In M. Munitz and P. Unger eds., *Semantics and Philosophy*. New York: New York University Press, pp. 197–213.

Stalnaker, R. (1997) 'Reference and Necessity.' In C. Wright and B. Hale eds., *Blackwell Companion to the Philosophy of Language*. Oxford: Blackwell: 534–54.

Stanley, J. and Z. Szabó (2000) 'On Quantifier Domain Restriction.' *Mind and Language* 15:219–61.

Strawson, P. (1950) 'On Referring.' *Mind* **59**. Reprinted in *Logico-Linguistic Papers*. London: Methuen, 1971, pp. 1–27.

Strawson, P. (1952) *Introduction to Logical Theory*. London: Methuen.

Strawson, P. (1959) *Individuals*. London: Methuen.

Strawson, P. (1964) 'Identifying Reference and Truth-Values.' *Theoria* **30**. Reprinted in *Logico-Linguistic Papers*. London: Methuen, 1971, pp. 75–95.

Bibliography

Szabó Z. (1999) 'Expressions and their Representations.' *Philosophical Quarterly* **49**, 145–63.

Szabó Z. (forthcoming a) 'Compositionality and Supervenience.' *Linguistics and Philosophy.*

Szabó Z. (forthcoming b) 'Descriptions and Uniqueness.' *Philosophical Studies.*

Szabó, Z. (forthcoming c) 'Adjectives in Context' R. Hamish and I. Kenesei eds., *Festschrift for Ferenc Kiefer.* Amsterdam: John Benjamins.

Thomson, J. (1992) 'On Some Ways in Which a Thing Can Be Good.' *Social Philosophy & Policy* **9**, No.2., pp. 96–117.

Thomson, J. (1994) 'Goodness and Utilitarianism.' *Proceedings of the American Philosophical Association* **67**, No.4., pp. 7–22.

Travis, C. (1994) 'On Constraints of Generality.' In *Proceedings of the Aristotelian Society. New Series,* **44**. London: Aristotelian Society Publications, pp. 165–88.

Westerståhl, D. (1998) 'On Mathematical Proofs of the Vacuity of Compositionality.' *Linguistics and Philosophy* **21**: 635–643.

Wettstein, H. (1981) 'Demonstrative Reference and Definite Descriptions.' *Philosophical Studies* **40**, pp. 241–57.

Wettstein, H. (1983) 'The Semantic Significance of the Referential-Attributive Distinction.' Reprinted in *Has Semantics Rested on a Mistake?* Palo Alto: Stanford University Press, pp. 50–8.

Wilson, G. (1991) 'Reference and Pronomial Descriptions.' *Journal of Philosophy* **88**, pp. 359–87.

Zadrozny, W. (1994) 'From Compositional to Systematic Semantics.' *Linguistics and Philosophy* **17**, pp. 329–42.

Zeevat, H. (1989) 'Realism and Definiteness.' In G. Chierchia, et al. eds., *Properties, Types and Meaning, vol. 2.* Dordrecht: Kluewer, pp. 269–97.

Ziff, P. (1960) *Semantic Analysis.* Ithaca: Cornell University Press.

Ziff, P. (1974) 'The Number of English Sentences.' *Foundations of Language* **11**, pp. 519–32.

Index

adjective(s), 96, 132, 150
   cluster, **107–8**, 109, 112,
   incomplete, **106–11**
   relative, **108**, 109, 110, 111
   scalar, **106–7**, 109, 110, 112
ambiguity, 88, 89, **91n.6**, 97
   semantic, 28–9, 128
   structural, 53n, 89
autonomy of syntax, 13

Bach, K., 130n.30
Bedeutung, 39
Berkeley, G., 128
Bloomfield. *See* Bloomfield's
   problem
Bloomfield's challenge. *See*
   Bloomfield's problem
Bloomfield's problem, 30–1,
   37, 46, 54, 56n.28, 149

Carnap, R., 11n.21
Chomsky, N., 40, 106n.26
compositionality:
   formulations of the principle
   of, **3**, 6–7, 9, 13n, **25**, 149-
   150

See also functionality,
   meaning(s): third dogma
   about, novelty: argument
   from, parallelism,
   substitutivity, understanding:
   argument from
content:
   assertoric, **70**, 70n.9, 72n.13
   cognitive, **65–7**
   referential, **65–7**
context, 101, 104–5, 109, 113,
   115, 117, 121, 123, 127,
   133, 136, 147, 150
   -dependency, **87**, 91–5, 99,
   107, 109, 112, 123, 131–4,
   150
      lexical, **90–1**, 113
      metalinguistic, **89–90**,
      91, 93, 113
      thesis, 87–95, 92n, 105, 117,
      123, 147, 150
      formulation of, 91

Davidson, D., 81–4
Davies, M., 132n.31

demonstratives, 118, 119n.8, 121

description(s), 28–9, 40, 102, **115–47**, 150
  definite, 28–9, 29n.4, 77n.20, 117n.5, 119, 120, 120n.12, 122, 122n.16, 124, 124n, 125n.20, 126n.21, 130, 130n.30, 139n.38, 140, 143
    attributive uses of, 121, 124
    context-dependency of, 131–4
    and file-cards, 126–8, 143–4
    and pragmatic coreference theory, 135–40, 137n.35
    referential uses of, 121, 124, 129
    incomplete, **131**
  indefinite, 120nn.11, 12., 121, 123n, 125n.20, 126n.22, 139n.38
    and file-cards, 126, 144
    and pragmatic coreference theory, 135, 138, 139
  theory of:
    broad sense, **118**,
    narrow sense, **118**,
determiner(s), **117–8**, 119n.8, 121, 132
determination, 4, **5–6**, 12n.24, 15, 15n.28, 21–5, 21n, 32, 34, 41n, 41–3, 44n, 45, 52, 53, 61, 64, 65–6, 74, 89, 105, 121, 122n.16, 123
  See also supervenience
Discourse Representation Theory (DRT), 4n.2, 125n.20

Donnellan, K., 121, 123–4, 128–9, 129n.27, 130, 137, 146
Dummett, M., 44–5, 45n.16, 48n, 59–62, 67, 70, 73

epistemology, 28, 46–8, 49, 51, 56
Evans, G., 140
  and MacDowell, J., 45n.16
external anchor, **135n.33**

Field, H., 30n.7
file-cards, 125–8, 135–9, 143–146, 146n.46
  See also semantics: file-change; theory: pragmatic coreference (PCT)
Fine, K., 18n
Fodor, J. and Sag, I., 121
Frawley, W., 54n.26
Frege, G., 6n.5, 7, 8n.13, 9, 10n.19, 12, 40, 59, 64–5, 73–5
  -an sense(s), 8n.13, 9–10, 42, 44–5, 45n.16, 59, 64–5, 73
    first criterion of difference for, **64**,
    second criterion of difference for, **65**
  -an thought(s), 9–10, 59
  -'s principle, 7, 59, 73n.16
functionality, **19–25**
  formulation of principle of, 19

Geach, P., 98–9, 99n.16, 103–104, 115
Grice, P., 112, 128, 138–9

Index

163

Heim, I., 125–8, 125n.20,
126n.22, 130–4, 134,
139n.38, 144–5, 146
Higginbotham, J., 106n.26
Hintikka, J., 12n.23
Hume, D., 83

identification:
of a particular object, **140**,
143
story-relative, **140–1**
incomplete predicate, 104, 105–
106, 109, 113
See also adjective(s):
incomplete
indexicals, 92n
idiom, 20, 20n.37, 21n

Kamp, H., 4n.2, 106n.26,
125n.20, 145
Kaplan, D., 10n.18
-'s character, 10n.18
-'s content, 10n.18
Karttunen, L., 126n.22
Kim, J., 22–4
Kripke, S., 28, 47, 70n.8,
122n.16, 128–9, 129n.27,
130, 146

Lakoff, G., 50n
Landeman, F., 146n.46
Lewis, D., 16n.29, 145,
146n.47
Leibniz, G. W., 34n.43
logical:
categories, 96
form(s), **96–102**, 99n.15,
104, 105–6, 106n, 112, 115,
116, 117n.4, 126, 127, 131,

142, 144–5, 146n.46, 147,
150
Lockwood, M., 143

Martin, R. L., 81n.23
meaning(s), **4–5**, 5n
and understanding, 64–7
identity conditions of, 37, 46
first dogma about, **32–9**, 44,
46
formulation of, 35
second dogma about, **39–46**,
64, 65, 66, 85, 92n, 122n.16
formulation of, 41
third dogma about, **52–6**, 54
See also semantic: value(s)
Meinong, A., 116, 119
Millikan, R., 126n.22
modality, 5, 6n.4, 21–5, 32,
33n, 41, 70, 70n.9, 92, 102
Montague, R., 11n.21
Moore, G. E., 23, 29, 98,
98n.13, 104
Mostowski, A., 140

Neale, S., 116–7, 116n.3,
117n.4
novelty, 74
argument from, **74–80**

ontology, 28, 30, 35–9, 49–52,
56, 101n.19

parallelism, **9–14**
phrase(s):
coreferring, **127–8**, 136,
140–6, 141, 143
quantifying, **120**, 121, 131–
134, 136, 140, 141, 143

164 Index

referring, **119**, 121, 136, 140, 141, 143

possible human language, 3, 3n, 23–5, 23n, 25n, 33, 33n, 34, 34n, 54, 74, 91, 92, 149

pragmatic(s), 38, 99, 128. *See also* theory: pragmatic coreference (PCT)

principle:
familiarity, **126**, 126n.21, 141
  and pragmatic coreference theory, 134–40, 135nn.33, 34.
novelty, **126**,
  and pragmatic coreference theory, 134–40, 135n.34, 139n.38,
of parallelism:
strong, **10–11**, 10n.18, 14
weak, **12**, 14
See also Frege: -'s principle; Russell: -'s principle

properties:
constitution, 22–5, 22n.39
etymological, 32–4
logical, 96
meaning, 22–5, 35
moral, 23–4
phonological, 32–4
physical, 23–4
semantic, **33–5**, 52
syntactic, 32–4

Putnam, H., 55–6, 65–6

quantifier(s), 118, **119–20**, 121, 132
domain, 33n, 116, 131–4, 137n.35, 141

quotation, **88n**

Quine, W. V., 35–8, 60n, 116, 116n.2, 142

Récanati, F., 137n.35

Reimer, M., 132

role:
and context, 104, **104n.24**
and meaning, 4, **5**

Russell, B., 28–9, 47, 116, 117n.5, 119, 122, 123, 142
-ian expansion, 120
-ian proposition(s), 10, 28, 124
-'s principle, 140

Sag, I. *See* Fodor, J. and Sag, I.

semantic(s):
descriptive, **47–8**, 49
  hypothetical, **50**
empirical, 50n
file-change, **125–8**, 144
foundational, **48**
intensional, 11–12
linguistic, 27–57, **31–2**, 47, 50–2, 54–5, 101–2, 149
methodology of, **27–30**, 31, 43
philosophical, **32**
possible worlds, 11–2, 34.
See also modality
subject matter of, 27, 30–1
value(s), **34–5**, 38–9, 41, 44, 45, 46n.19, 46–7, 48, 49, 51, 53, 54, 55, 98–100

sense(s):
ingredient, **70**, 70n.9, 72nn. 12, 13.
See also Frege: -an sense(s)

sensitivity to surroundings, **77**

Index

165

Sinn. *See* Frege: -an sense
Stalnaker, R., 20n.37, 47–8
Strawson, P., 124n, 140–2
structure, 4, **5**, 5n, 6, 9, 11, 18–19, 22, 36, 54–6, 59, 61–4, 80
  grammatical, 90n.3
  logical. *See* logical: form(s)
structural conditionals, **54**
substitutivity, **14–9**, 14n, 19n.34
  formulation of the principle of, 14
supervenience, 150
  strong, 24–5, 42, 42n, 122n.16
    formulation of, 24
  weak, 22–4, 25, 122n.16
    formulation of, 22
synonymy, 5, 9n.15, 16–8, 19, 20, 22, 23n, 37–9, 97

Tarski, A., 127
terms:
  O-, **145**
  T-, **145–6**
theory:
  ambiguity, 129
  coreferential theory. *See* theory: pragmatic coreference (PCT)

either-or, **121**
neither-nor, **121–2**
pragmatic coreference (PCT), **134–46**, 135n.33, 137n.35, 140, 142–3
quantificational, **119–20**, 121, 122–8, 129, 133, 137n.35, 138–9
  in a fixed context, 132
referential, **118–9**, 121, 122, 122n.16
Travis, C., 92–5, 105, 112, 113

understanding, 62–63, 66
  argument from, **59–64**, 74, 80, 149
  principle of:
    modest, **60–3**, 66, 73–80, 84, 85
    strong, **60–3**, 66, 67–73, 85
    weak, **84**, 84n.30, 85

vague(ness), 37–8, 43, 94, 112

Zadrozny, W., 5n
Zeevat, H., 143
Ziff, P., 111n